T0105688

Window
to Eternity

Window *to* Eternity

Edgar L. Biamonte

BALBOA.
PRESS
A DIVISION OF HAY HOUSE

Balboa Press books may be ordered through booksellers or by contacting:

Balboa Press
A Division of Hay House
1663 Liberty Drive
Bloomington, IN 47403
www.balboapress.com
1-(877) 407-4847

Because of the dynamic nature of the Internet, any web addresses or links contained in this book may have changed since publication and may no longer be valid. The views expressed in this work are solely those of the author and do not necessarily reflect the views of the publisher, and the publisher hereby disclaims any responsibility for them.

The author of this book does not dispense medical advice or prescribe the use of any technique as a form of treatment for physical, emotional, or medical problems without the advice of a physician, either directly or indirectly. The intent of the author is only to offer information of a general nature to help you in your quest for emotional and spiritual well-being. In the event you use any of the information in this book for yourself, which is your constitutional right, the author and the publisher assume no responsibility for your actions.

Certain stock imagery © Thinkstock.
Any people depicted in stock imagery provided by Thinkstock are models, and such images are being used for illustrative purposes only.

ISBN: 978-1-4525-4490-8 (e)
ISBN: 978-1-4525-4491-5 (sc)
ISBN: 978-1-4525-4492-2 (hc)

Library of Congress Control Number: 2012903651

Printed in the United States of America

Balboa Press rev. date: 05/01/2012

Contents

Part II
Autobiography

Part III
The Paranormal and Related Spiritual Concepts

Foreword

Window to Eternity discusses the meaning of life and that life continues after death. It supersedes and encompasses most books on life/death matters, and is important to those who fear that death ends all, or, if not, that they're destined to suffer forever in hell as punishment for so-called sins. Nor would a loving Creator do so, which would be immoral.

Religions, odd philosophies, superstitions, fearful notions and so on, have clouded our minds and prevented us from understanding our purpose here, not our Creator.

This is the learning and rejecting plane, which is one of the book's major themes. God has deliberately arranged this unusual stage, which is a material world that contains objects—things. They offer *us* a chance to choose between sharing and giving, instead of hoarding and taking, for example, concepts that we cannot learn or reject in a spiritual dimension that lacks anything material. Nor can we learn about the peculiarity of killing one another (or not), except here, since nothing physical exists there either.

After death, the essence of us, our souls, joins other souls in heaven or the spiritual dimension, two labels which this writer uses interchangeably throughout the book.

Physical life isn't meaningless, as agnostics, atheists, and particularly those who suffer more than others, often contend. Were this true, God would be superficial and even cruel for having fashioned such a negative, contradictory scenario, which is impossible considering that God created an incredible, clock-running universe and heaven, which It is holding together *lovingly* (in human terms). Were It not doing so *lovingly*, all would collapse including God and us.

The book also contends that there's no evidence that God interferes in our lives. Were this true, the Creator would have long since stopped wars, famines, and disasters, most of which *we* have caused and are still causing for many reasons, not God. Ironically, such interference would prevent us from choosing to learn to love one another and ourselves enough for us to handle such matters ourselves.

Window also maintains that although physical life forces us to depend on our parents, then employers and others later on, we will not be obligated to group with such souls after arriving in heaven, but, rather, with souls with whom we are morally and spiritually compatible, just as we did here, beyond the family and others without realizing it.

As physical beings living in this material dimension, most of us tune in to the physical aspect of ourselves, not the intangible, spiritual part, or the soul, which leaves us after physical death and enters heaven afterwards.

Idol worshipping, ritualism, and mumbling rote words, et cetera, have also clouded our purpose here, not God. Despite the glitter, gadgets, and toys (for young and old) that distract us, the challenge in a capitalistic world, is to be much more loving (than we think we are), which is a positive energy force we must take into the next world in order to prevent negative souls from overcoming the loving, positive souls there. Failing would cause the same collapse, as previously stated.

Hopefully the book will prevent others from fearing death or punishment from the Creator, as some religions maintain, and thereby help them make the proper transition to the next world instead of lingering here as ghosts.

Personal note from the author

Throughout the book, I have attempted to theorize my personal conception of God, that is, the Ultimate force or energy (which I often refer to as *It* in order to avoid *He*, since, whatever God is called, such as It, Ala, or Jehovah, the Creator couldn't have a gender.

The book contains three parts. The first refers to my conception of God, physical life, death, and the nature of heaven, the spiritual dimension. The second is autobiographical, pertaining to how I arrived at such conclusions after experiencing what many might consider the paranormal. The last refers to those very paranormal incidents that I experienced which relate to this book, and includes my evaluation of reincarnation, demons, and related spiritual concepts.

All the incidents presented here are factual, even the dialogue, which I mention because, contrary to traditional belief, factual writing has much more power and impact than fiction. Furthermore, I have been writing and re-writing for many years, even took notes, and can remember incidents going back to first grade, including most of my peers' names.

Very early in life, I became involved and fascinated with metaphysics. Deep within my psyche, I even envisioned writing this book and others, which appeared to be my destiny. Basically a loner, I sensed that taking drugs would prevent me from evaluating physical life and the afterlife *naturally*, which I believe is the only way to do so correctly and honestly.

Nor did I want to risk jeopardizing my health with poison. Though some jazz musicians claim that doing drugs improves their playing, while striving, that is, practicing to become a quality jazz pianist, as I will describe in Part II, I was always skeptical. On the contrary, I was convinced that I could do better naturally, which I accomplished years ago after overcoming attention deficit disorder and other problems during my youth. In fact, I had some very *natural*, supposedly paranormal experiences doing so.

I avoided footnoting information because I didn't want to turn this book into a documented thesis. Besides, I knew that footnoting what near/death individuals *supposedly* experienced after *supposedly* visiting heaven could hardly provide undeniable proof that that dimension *really* exists. Also, since we're all in this together, I decided to write in an informal, friendly, self-revealing, personal style.

Acknowledgment

I dedicate this book to my four children who remained faithful and loving toward me and discussed many controversial issues that I raise in this book.

I appreciate that Doug Beauchamp, an artist and arranger, was kind enough to read a recent version of this book, and make several constructive suggestions.

Preface

Considering the *Bible*, the *Koran*, philosophies, and countless religions, which often disagree with one another, I can understand why some people reject God altogether.

"Who cares? Why get stressed out trying to figure all that out?" a female agnostic once protested to me. "I'm happy to be with my grandchildren and that's it."

That's her choice, I thought, but when she added, "You must be constantly upset trying to figure all that out," I disagreed inwardly.

Delving into such mysteries (metaphysics) is challenging and fascinating. What could be more important than trying to figure out life's meaning and a possible afterlife? Many of us think this is beyond our ability, arrogant, and even sacrilegious, though philosophers and religious leaders have been struggling to do just that, since civilization's beginning.

Living in the country years ago, I befriended a nearby farmer who never checked the news on television or in the newspaper. He lived a simple life centered on raising and milking his cows, which I respected, especially since he was kind, just, and honest, which supersedes so many serious faults. But I'd rather find myself stressed searching for the light, than content sitting in the dark.

I've spent a lifetime struggling to understand life and death. In this book, I theorize why a supreme power and intelligence must exist, and why It created the universe, the spiritual world (heaven), and man. Analyzing the accounts of numerous near/death victims who supposedly glimpsed the spiritual world (heaven) and returned, I have pieced together—imagined—what the spiritual world is like, which might sound unscientific and speculative. But we shouldn't underestimate the imagination, which we have used to advance from caveman days to our present modern civilization. Having never been to the Caribbean Islands or seen pictures of them, *imagining* palm trees, white sand, and beautiful blue water surrounding the islands, we can *imagine* what they're like, true about heaven.

Nor are my conclusions drug induced, which I don't do other than occasional alcohol, and I have never smoked anything. Though some drugs like LSD, ecstasy, and others seem to alter perception, which supposedly enables some to experience unusual visions, such as alien contact or momentary departures into other dimensions, so what? I have always wondered, other than possibly providing pleasurable highs and brief escapes from troubles and stress. Such individuals still have to return to this plane and face their problems (unless they overdose and pass on).

PART I

God, Physical Life and Death,
and the Nature of Heaven

CHAPTER 1

Problems Understanding and Communicating with God

CONFLICTING CONCEPTIONS ABOUT SPIRITUAL MATTERS have disturbed many of us for decades, particularly the religiously faithful. The major problem is that although evidence is lacking that God really answers our prayers or helps us in any way, many are unconvinced and even offer personal examples as proof that the opposite is true. The point is, God would be unjust, if It only answered some prayers but not all, or saved one sick person's life and not another's, or stopped one war and not another, and so on. If God *did* answer our prayers, most of us would pray to become materially wealthy, which is spiritually worthless, teaches us nothing, and would hardly prepare us for the next world. In fact, answering individual prayers would probably cause jealousy, hatred, anger, and even more wars and suffering.

Many disbelievers complain that the Creator has not eliminated worldwide pain and suffering, especially from war, genocide, disease, and famines or from natural disasters like earthquakes, hurricanes, tsunamis, and others. How come God didn't intercede during the holocaust? Jews and others often protest.

God does not seem to inspire or reward the good, who often leave us too soon, many also complain. Though God supposedly spoke to man through angels, according to the *Bible*, why doesn't God do so, today? others often wonder. Consequently, many have left the church, have become atheists or agnostics, or follow nothing.

Whether or not most religious leaders truly believe that God does interfere in our lives is material. The point is, that most preach that *He* does or they urge their flock to have faith that *He* does, which confuses many when their prayers go unanswered.

Despite God's obvious non-interference, another problem is that many religious leaders also urge their flock to love God with all their heart and soul, which is difficult, much like asking us to love the indifferent, that is, a God that seems to ignore us. Loving such an entity can only spring from those who struggle to understand such an abstract unknown. Nor can much love spring from the suffering, maladjusted, and discontent (for whatever reason), but, rather, from the mature and well adjusted or from monks and others who spend hours doing so through meditation.

Though most believers are secretly indebted to It for having created the material world and life, leaders also ask their followers to pray to this unknown, including kneeling, bowing, and other physical quirks, mostly from inside certain buildings, as if God particularly appreciates groups doing so inside sheltered areas and because of countless other reasons which *we* have concocted, not God, once again.

Sometimes we feel guilty about our difficulty to love God, which some religions consider sinful. But trying to love such an awesome Supreme Intelligence is like trying to love something intangible like electricity, fusion, or the sun's energy. We have trouble loving one another, much less such an awesome, indefinable power.

Another problem is that many of us never indulged in passionate, exhausting discussions about the nature of our God. Or, if we did, we were dissatisfied with answers or conclusions, which were often contradictory or seemed unanswerable. Giving up, many stuck to flawed, inherited religion, or became agnostics or atheists. (Whatever the case, most important is that whatever force or energy is responsible for creating the spectacular universe and spiritual dimension, cannot be stupid and/or immoral, and discussions leading to those conclusions are erroneous.)

Some weren't curious enough to dig deeply and evaluate what theologians and philosophers have said about metaphysics, either, and still aren't. Others are too lazy, disinterested, or too involved with their hectic physical lives to bother. Many think that physical life is the real world anyway, and/or that life ends after physical death.

Agnostics, atheists and others also contend that God behaves so mysteriously, that knowing It, that is, delving into Its essence, or comprehending Its force or energy, is impossible for lowly humans, another reason why they reject God.

Nevertheless, though we have difficulty understanding, knowing, or connecting with this incredible intelligence (including disappointment and even anger that It doesn't communicate with us), deep inside our psyche or subconscious, I suspect that most of us, including even atheists and agonistics, sense that God *does* indeed exist. This isn't just my wishful thinking or because disbelievers secretly fear God's wrath if they disbelieve, but, rather, because we're all infinitesimal, spiritual aspects of It, as the *Bible* maintains.

That our Creator would need and/or demand that we pray to It, including with uplifted hands supposedly pointing up to It (as if God resides in the universe), is like the sun's energy needing the same. Since reaching or communicating with God, seems impossible from here, we can only speculate how much we can *really* know about what It needs from us.

Such religious ritualism bothered me throughout my early life. Mellowing, years later, I concluded that if repeating rote words, gesticulating, kissing idols, drinking wine, getting submerged in water (including bathing, drinking, and urinating in the polluted Ganges), thumping chests and whatnot (The list is endless), calms certain people, strengthens their belief in God and provides hope about an afterlife, that's their choice, which I respect. Unlike in the past, many countries allow religious freedom today, that is, their leaders brainwash the masses into following what they impose upon them.

Assuming that we could reach this force, energy, or intelligence we call God, or we could somehow communicate with It, then what? I have also always wondered. Would we continue to beg or demand that It help us solve personal and worldwide problems, which *we* have mostly created? Would we scold It for ignoring us in the past? Or would we continue asking It to help us acquire more and more material things?

God refusing to answer our prayers to spare us, and/or love ones from injuries, sicknesses such as cancer and death, often causes disappointment and sometimes even anger. Considering the many odd cases of those who survive disasters, plane crashes, and so on, doesn't prove that the Creator interfered in their behalf, but, rather, that we will die when it is our time. This doesn't mean that God would stop a bullet intended for someone if it wasn't that person's time. Possibly through a premonition, that person would have a near-death experience and survive, or would somehow manage to avoid that scenario entirely. In other words, *we,* not God, seem to control when we will turn ourselves off, sometimes even under what circumstances, such as whether peacefully, through suffering, or even what might seem like accidentally. During long periods of sickness or aging, many individuals even know precisely when they will terminate, which suggests that we're really in control. *We* also seem to be in charge of our own individual destinies, not God, which seems logical.

Though many of us pray for peace, *we* are capable of achieving it, if every single soul truly believed and followed it with his heart and soul, unconditionally, consistently, and lovingly. The problem is that we haven't advanced to that point yet.

Professional sport players and others who look up or point to the sky (suggesting that God exists somewhere here), then thanking It for helping them perform well at something as trivial as baseball or football, is wishful thinking. It suggests that our Creator is equally as trivial, which is impossible considering that It created the complicated physical and spiritual worlds.

Natural disasters seem to be part of our scenario in order to offer us the chance to become loving enough to prevent them (when possible) and truly helping the victims afterwards, which we failed to do concerning Katrina. Many people would have survived. Had politicians and rescue leaders possessed enough love before and after this tragedy.

We're slow about controlling pollution and its damaging effect on our ozone layer because most world leaders don't care enough about one another to stop haggling and *really* do something positively and quickly about it. The greenhouse effect appears to be worsening our weather, possibly even causing more hurricanes, tornados, and storms than necessary, which is because of *our* indifference, once again, not God's.

We know where the earth's faults lie. Most likely scientists will soon be able to predict when and where earthquakes and volcanoes will occur. Surely a God that created the universe and life is capable of stopping them, which would teach us nothing again. Instead, God has left us with the challenge of caring enough about ourselves and others to move away from such potential danger spots.

Only recently have we placed detectors on buoys in order to warn us against tsunamis. We could conceivably reduce or eliminate famines, diseases, and more if we *really* cared enough about one another (and ourselves).

Looking back to my high school years, I remember my inspiring English teacher, Ms. Wilkinson, who had us memorize the following, famous lines from Shakespeare's *Hamlet*:

> Out, out brief candle, life is but a walking shadow, a poor player who frets upon the stage and is heard no more. It is a tale told by an idiot, full of sound and fury signifying nothing.

Though I didn't understand the meaning until years later, I accept that we are actors on a stage which is our planet, but disagree that life is meaningless. We are involved with a non-interfering God that has set a stage, which includes natural disasters, evilness, happiness and joy, and much more.

Were God immoral, It would behave like immoral humans, like hackers who infest computers with viruses for "the fun of it." In the same sense, It would have long since played games with us, like tampering with gravity, electricity, or whatever laws It created, causing explosions and chaos. Nor would we or the spiritual world exist, had It chosen to do so.

Considering that our universe functions perfectly, that is, laws work beautifully, consistently, and seemingly endlessly, our Creator *must* exist and *must* be morally perfect beyond reproach (true about other Gods if they exist.) There's no other possibility. Furthermore, we should strive to do likewise, because, as reflections of It, we are capable of following suit on an infinitesimal level.

Nor would our morally perfect God have created a chaotic spiritual world. Surely it contains predictable laws that differ from ours here, which we will need to follow after arriving there.

Feeling guilty about not getting to know or love God is an unnecessary and an unwise burden to maintain here and take into the next world. That such a fantastic power would punish us in any way (after having created us physically and morally imperfect), such as sending us to a horrible domain called hell to suffer forever for so-called sins, would suggest an immoral Creator.

CHAPTER 2

Proof that God Exists

WHETHER OR NOT "GOD IS, was, and always will be;" whether or not It evolved or another intelligence created It, seems less important than attempting to prove Its' existence. I speculate that It exists, but not as a huge, accessible mass somewhere in our universe where contact is possible. Were that true, we could probably do so. Wherever It exists, which is obviously in another dimension such as heaven, rather than here, It is obviously unobservable and difficult to know, as we might know a friend or loved one.

To prove that God exists, one need only consider the universe. Surely a super intelligence must have created such a spectacular panorama of mass and energy that includes gravity, electricity, fusion, and much more. Also, the universe functions beautifully and consistently, which we can count on to do today, tomorrow, and as long as our planet exists, providing we don't destroy it through atomic warfare or the effects of pollution.

Mostly negative, the media tries to capture our attention for profit. Surely a lethal asteroid could hit our planet and destroy us, if that is our destiny according to the Creator's plan. But having created us for a purpose, why would God allow this to happen? which would be comparable to us planning our children's demise for misbehaving. In other words, having possibly struggled to become such an infinite force, which is beyond our imagination, surely It would enable (inspire) *us* to avoid this, which scientists and others are working to prevent today.

Mountains don't fly off the earth one day, then somehow return and bombard us the next. Engines don't start one day and suddenly explode indiscriminately on another, as if the Supreme Being were immoral. Thanks to our scientists again, whatever we cannot understand or whatever seems contradictory about how it functions, they often unravel and explain later.

We plant seeds and they germinate. Absorbing minerals and something called *water and photosynthesis,* plants grow, which I consider amazing. Some stretch into huge plants (trees) whose leaves absorb carbon dioxide and release oxygen which sustains physical life. Leaves eventually flutter to the ground according to something called gravity. They ultimately rot and provide food for that very tree, which is also incredible. Most trees sleep for a spell, wake up, and the cycle repeats itself at different times throughout the planet, according to the weather, which varies because the earth tilts, allowing the sun to heat different areas throughout the year, which is also equally remarkable.

Though plants die, they're capable of reseeding, which prevents the species from disappearing. If reproduction weren't part of our picture or suddenly stopped, life would perish. Though many of us take all this for granted, everything seems to have been carefully planned, particularly the balance in nature between animals, insects, and plant life. This balance manages to prevail, despite our irresponsible, interference, and negligence, which includes killing off animals (instead of eating plants, fruit, and nuts, et cetera, which would seem more logical for many reasons.)

More incredible are cells that divide and duplicate, rather than die and vanish. Sperm enter the ovum and ultimately produce a baby that will grow, and what is this *growing* that allows plants and a child to mature, stretch into something different?

That so many different, complicated life forms exist, particularly man, suggests that some great intelligence initiated everything, which we rarely consider because most of us focus on making money and collecting material things. Because a spiritual dimension awaits us after death, the challenge in a mostly capitalistic environment is for us to be less materialistic and more spiritual and certainly loving.

"All this is the nature," my first wife constantly insisted, because she was basically an atheist.

"But what is nature, except another label for our Creator?" I always answered.

That we're susceptible to cancer and other terrible diseases, might suggest an unloving or non-existent God. But evaluating this objectively and broadmindedly (instead of personally and emotionally), to repeat, the Creator has obviously chosen *not* to interfere, which we should accept, even if only because we have no other choice.

Apparently, the Creator has arranged our scenario so that although we can slow aging, we cannot live forever, as we know. What isn't so obvious *but extremely important,* is that since the Creator cannot be immoral, It has also allowed diseases to exist, so that, once again, *we* can choose to care enough to help ourselves and others overcome them, or not. What other logical, moral reason could there be?

We are mostly responsible for causing diseases, *not God,* possibly even true about those we inherit. Ironically, however, this is like another *Catch-22*. We need to suffer from diseases and evilness in order to learn the opposite—concepts such as happiness and goodness.

We inherit many different diseases, as most of us know. But not loving ourselves and others enough to stop environmental pollution, smoking, obesity, drinking alcohol, and so on, is compounding the problem. Because most food companies are concerned about profits, not if their products cause cancer, they try to circumvent the Food and Drug Administration's controls about the hormones they inject into cattle (to fatten them) and the insecticides they use to preserve crops.

Ironically, in all fairness to them, they would fold, and would therefore lay off employee who wouldn't be able to earn money in order to buy their infected cattle and crops (and eventually die from cancer). Fortunately, many good souls sell the healthiest, poison-free food possible.

Many of us might wonder why a supposedly loving God created us susceptible to death, which disappoints and frightens us, especially if we're unsure that life continues afterwards. Believing that it does, should alleviate such fears and enable us to evaluate our picture differently. Whatever was Its reason for creating us, God has given us the chance to enjoy physical life—a great gift—why most of us, even those suffering from unavoidable handicaps, wish to live as long as possible.

CHAPTER 3

We're Part Spiritual in Nature like God

ACCORDING TO OUR DIMENSION'S LAWS, when possible, we're capable of transporting, rearranging, and transforming material into what befits our needs, even according to our deepest desires. Using machinery, which we have constructed from the planet's resources, we move mountains, build reservoirs, and redirect rivers, et cetera. We have created physical things (from a simple shed to a city), individually, or collectively, some of us with more skill and success than others.

Physical life is real, not a dream, as some philosophers considered. Yet, paradoxically, since our desires spring from dreams, physical life seems dreamlike. I speculate that this dreamlike, reflective, or imaginative quality is our spiritual aspect, which is similar, on a small scale, to what motivated the Creator to develop and eventually create heaven and the universe. Various kinds of serious meditation (rather than rote), can help us tune in to our spiritual aspect.

Differentiating between this physical and spiritual aspect is simple but important. Sports, like playing baseball, football, and golf, requires mostly our physical aspect. Anything related to deep reasoning, reflection, and particularly creative thinking, requires our spiritual side. Physically learning how to hold a pen, pencil, or manipulating the computer keyboard is easy. Learning how to write coherently and master the language is more difficult and can take a lifetime. This is true about writing successful and meaningful poetry (as opposed to verse) or literary books (instead of trash), which requires deep reflection.

Mental suffering, which involves our spiritual aspect, is more painful than physical, especially if long-lasting, but infinitesimal compared to what the Creator must have endured struggling to evolve and create our universe and spiritual dimension.

Serious, dedicated artists (rather than those who prostitute their souls for money), often feel close to the Creator because they too create something from nothing. In my case, I first contemplated the idea of this book as a spark of intention, which first evolved (from mental and spiritual energy) until it grew, developed, and became this book.

As a professional jazz pianist, I use my fingers, the physical aspect of myself, to improvise what I think and feel which stems from my spiritual or mental side, particularly when I play slow, emotional ballads. At the risk of sounding immodest, my ideas appear to be improving or evolving, that is, reaching a more advanced state.

Reaching my present level of piano improvisation, took years, not just because I had to learn how to finger properly and advance technically (the physical aspect) or because practicing for hours can be boring, tedious, and lonesome, but because, as an abused child with attention deficit disorder and other problems, I had difficulty developing my spiritual aspect until years later.

CHAPTER **4**

Theorizing How God Evolved

WHY THE UNIVERSE DIDN'T JUST suddenly appear; why it seemed to arrive as a Big Bang (According to some scientists, reverberations are still detected in the universe's outer reaches), is difficult to explain because how It accomplished this incredible feat is beyond our comprehension. Like many of us who suffer through physical life (but, again, microscopically, compared to how much the Creator could be suffering because we're still killing one another off and for many other reasons), we can hardly imagine what spiritual upheavals, dilemmas, or catastrophes It had to experience before reaching Its' present level of energy and intelligence (for lack of any other words to describe Its essence.) Though we have difficulty knowing such an entity, one which probably doesn't need our sympathy, It is surely worthy of our praise and love for having created such a splendid universe and us.

"Who created God?" I recall asking a professor, while I attended college.

"Probably another God, and another God created that God, ad infinitum, forming some kind of circle, each God feeding, sustaining, and enhancing one another," he answered, which I have paraphrased.

Interesting, I thought then. But I have my own theory, which I remember considering at about age eight, which I will mention not to impress the reader, but because the closer we are to when we left the spiritual world, the closer we are to recollecting what it was like. In fact, all of us seem capable of doing so (through various kinds of meditation), just as Emerson, Thoreau and the transcendendentalists believed. Were we capable of speaking well at age one or earlier (which might be possible some day), we might be able to describe the spiritual dimension with greater accuracy (than I'm attempting in this book), including the nature of God. Conversely, the older we get, the greater is the chance of forgetting both, especially because we're mostly concerned about money, material objects, raising our children, and whatever else is associated with physical life.

My theory about how God evolved involves picturing or meditating about the depth of infinity. If nothing happened throughout infinity, nothing would exist today, including us. But considering that the universe exists, plus life and us, proves that something *did* happen because both are here. Apparently, out of the depths of this nothingness and endlessness, some kind of spiritual awareness (or spiritual mutation) emerged which grew until It became the awesome Creator that created the spiritual world, our physical dimension and life. Nor can I accept that God first began materially and changed into something spiritual.

This something—a spiritual spark of awareness or intelligence—was God's beginning, Its birth. More difficult to explain in human terms, is how this microscopic spark developed and expanded into the awesome intelligence or energy that created both dimensions—quite an achievement considering that we can't create anything material from nothing.

Recognizing early in Its' development that doing nothing would have been negative and worthless, It chose to advance (much like how we have done similarly since our beginning, because, once again, coming from God, we're much like God.)

(That we might have descended from aliens who inhabited Earth thousands of years ago, is possible, but, if true, that doesn't explain what intelligence created the universe and spiritual world and why.)

At age three, nobody can build anything sophisticated, such as a shed, not just because we're physically incapable, but because our minds, our spiritual aspect, haven't matured enough to understand hammering, cutting wood, and measuring, or the reason for a door, windows, and a roof, et cetera.

Since our beginning, we have been using our planet's resources to improve our living condition. Today, according to our capitalistic system (that is, how God has set our stage), unless we're already wealthy, we must work in order to earn money to buy food and shelter for survival. But rather than remaining satisfied with the basics, most of us, including even those in the most primitive societies, desire to have more and better material things, from a better spear, to a better car or home. We desire to be much like God when, as a spiritual entity, It added the universe to Itself. In fact, again, much like God, many of us aspire to create replicas of ourselves—in the form of children.

CHAPTER 5

Evolutionism versus Creationalism

THAT WE DESCENDED FROM THE apes, according to Darwin, caused quite a sensation when his theory emerged. Many of us like myself accepted it because it was fashionable to do so, since rejecting it suggested refusal to keep up with the times, narrow-mindedness and even ignorance. But since there's no evidence that we evolved from the sea, became amphibious, and became an offshoot from the apes, nor have scientists found the so-called missing link, I reject that man evolved from the apes and accept creationalism, namely, that God placed man on Earth instantaneously, when the planet was capable of sustaining life. Nor could a God that created such awesome, complicated dimensions like the universe and heaven have trouble doing this.

I keep an open mind that aliens might be our ancestors or that they're curious about us. But since intelligence and love *must* rule advanced life (or such life wouldn't have advanced like us), despite our generally violent and primitive nature why wouldn't they reveal themselves to us, unless they're spiritual, why radar cannot detect them. Surely, we would, were we capable of reaching them.

Whether or not man emerged six thousand years ago according to the *Bible* is immaterial. Furthermore, God might have placed different creatures on earth at different intervals, including man and certainly *after* dinosaurs, not during, as Hollywood often portrays.

CHAPTER **6**

Speculating Why God Created Man

WHY GOD CREATED THE UNIVERSE and man, is the next question. Arguing that It did because It had nothing else to do, for amusement, or for other odd reasons that disbelievers often concoct, implies that God is superficial or stupid. In human terms, despite Its struggle, God most likely experienced great joy after managing to create both dimensions, much like how we feel after creating anything meaningful, from a sculpture to a luxury ship or city, despite the obstacles or challenge.

I theorize that our Creator has given us free will in order to develop, advance, and become highly moral and loving here, so that we can transport that love energy (whatever the label, once again) into heaven, which might somehow enhance our Creator or somehow enable It to prevail. Conversely, should we fail, that is, should evilness overcome the good, chaos would follow and God would cease to exist. (Despite criticizing humans for lacking deep love for one another and other problems that face us, which I will discuss later, the world contains too many decent humans for me to believe that mankind is basically evil.)

Unfortunately, throughout history up to today, males have been slaughtering one another for world power and other reasons. They have also been dominating women, whom God seems to have endowed with more love and nurturing than men, since they're the bearers of children. Had that role been given to men from our beginning, they would have probably passed it on to Mom anyway, (so they could have enough time to hack one another off at the battlefield, and the world would probably be half as populated or nonexistent today.)

To show off their masculinity, males, at an early age here in America (and possibly throughout the supposedly civilized world), seem to enjoy roughing up one another, generally speaking, including even girls, which, ironically, isn't the case in primitive cultures. Males seemingly transfer this inherent desire into such areas as sports, business, and/or the military.

CHAPTER 7

The Soul

THE KEY TO UNDERSTANDING OUR system of things, including God, is the soul. One of our species' most fascinating aspects, it is the essence of each human which is the spiritual or intangible part of us, our personality or psyche (however expressed), which differentiates us from others and separates us from animals.

The body is the soul's container, as philosophers, theologians, and others have maintained throughout history. Death frees the soul from this cumbersome tomb, and we grieve when love ones pass on. Needing closure, we usually bury them, then visit them, decomposing, or already decomposed in graves at cemeteries, which is illogical, since their essence—their souls—have separated and left for the spiritual world, an almost infinite dimension that superimposes, encompasses, and surrounds the material world and others, if they exist.

Souls, there, have difficulty returning here because of the differences in dimensions. Why would they, considering that heaven is far superior to the material world? If they manage to do so as ghosts or other forms, for whatever reason, they're incapable of injuring us physically as Hollywood sometimes portrays.

How much they can harm us, mentally, is questionable and depends on how receptive we are to such influences and other factors. Ironically, believing that possibility, often opens up the chance for them to do so, which I will also discuss later.

Though we have the opportunity to learn to be truly loving toward one another like the Creator is toward us (or we wouldn't exist), many of us don't *really* understand the concept. For example, the macho and chauvinistic contingent and others frequently suppress this emotion which they equate with sissies, homosexuals, and "needy woman," as some put it, all of whom, ironically, usually possess enough love to tolerate them.

Truly loving others beyond loving oneself, requires deep, uninhibited feelings, which some of us possess, but is hard to explain to others who lack the quality, especially the cold and indifferent. Nor can such individuals have deep love for the Creator.

Ironically, so blessed, loving souls frequently need to raise their shields (rather than the sword) against "those who couldn't care less" about anyone but themselves, a familiar phrase many disgruntled, misled teens expressed when I taught secondary school during the Sixties and later. Unfortunately, instead of "rising above" the injustice of the times and their own self-pity, many found themselves criticized because of their loose morals, rebellion against the Vietnam War and the establishment (and other reasons), and turned to drugs.

Apparently, God's system of things enables the soul to incarnate into a physical body the moment we're born. Craving food, attention, and relief from waste, we're selfish and demanding during this time. Receiving neither, a newborn often cries and sometimes screams. In fact, unless blessed with unusual perception early in life, we often carry selfishness into the difficult teenage years and late adulthood. Worse, if we never learn to truly love one another; that is, if we never rise above selfishness, greed, and jealousy during physical life (The list is endless, again), we could overload the spiritual world with such negativity, causing it to collapse, along with everything else, as I have stated.

CHAPTER 8

Idiosyncrasies and Purpose of our Material World

DURING CAVEMAN DAYS, FINDING A stone or choice branch to fashion into a spear or tool, which humans could hold or keep alongside while eating, sleeping, or hunting, meant ownership. This is still generally true about how we evaluate material objects today, which we think we own, especially since our laws uphold what we buy or have in our house, et cetera. But since we can't take anything with us after death, as we know, this is an illusion, philosophically speaking. (Even God doesn't *really* own the universe.) *Things* in our material world are simply objects, that is, bits of our planet. They enable us to build everything from gadgets to cities, mostly for our comfort, use, pleasure, and much more.

But God seems to have placed us in a world containing objects for another very important reason that explains why It created our material world. Here, depending on our age, maturity, temperament differences, intelligence, and other characteristics, particularly our love for others or lack of it, we learn how to respond to countless situations involving objects or things.

How we use and manipulate them (or not), offers us the chance (choice) to be givers, namely generous, loving and honest, which is positive, or takers, that is, the greedy, selfish, and so on, which is the negative attitude.

Here, we build something for ourselves or others, move objects from one place to another, or repair them, and so on, all of which we cannot accomplish in the next world. As givers, the concept of lending something to someone (or not) from a pen to a car or huge sums of money is another peculiarity confined to our plane.

Lending raises such questions as, if I do so, what should I expect in return? attention, a favor, love, sex, thanks, nothing? What has that person given me or my family before? a lender might question before doing so, which cannot be accomplished in the spiritual plane. Ironically, lending risks the chance that the object might be returned broken, or not at all, which concerns how much we care (or not) about ourselves, our family, or others.

We also can choose (or not) to be takers (the negative factor), that is, selfish, greedy, hoarders and much more, including being jealous of those who have more or better objects than we (even size often matters). Sometimes takers become angry enough to kill in order to "have" that which they lack or want to replace with something that they believe is superior.

"Time is money," we also say here, which are both non-existent there.

We can't tarnish, break, damage or have anything stolen there. Nor can we *utilize* or construct anything tangible, or *sacrifice* something in order to help or benefit another.

Only here can we learn to steal or not, since there's nothing to steal there. Thievery, from a pen to expensive objects, and/or money, affects the thief's soul and sometimes the victim's. Finding out, a victim might be angry enough to seek revenge, which is a state of mind (the spiritual aspect of ourselves), which we should overcome or leave behind before death. Those who steal even incidental things, carry that negativism into the spiritual world.

Borrowing anything, as the taker, is another concept confined to the peculiarity of this plane and opens up other issues. Recently, soloing on my keyboard for a small, outside wedding, I took a break and was the only one with a pen, which I loaned to a guest who needed it to sign something connected with the wedding. Sometime later, I asked for it back in order to correct some chords on a song the bride handed me to play, and was surprised when the borrower laughed about having lost it and shrugged it off without bothering to look for it.

No big deal, trivial, one might say, especially because pens are cheap, which is immaterial and not the issue. Treating another person badly *is*, which is never a good idea, despite how seemingly insignificant.

Here, to express our feelings, we can give someone a rose or any object, but not there. Such objects could convey forgiveness or sympathy, which is positive, but even sarcasm, which is negative, like sending someone a dead rat in the mail or something similar (as a joke or for whatever reason) which is unloving. Remaining angry, bitter, and mean until the end, also for whatever reason (instead of loving, which is positive), a soul could carry such qualities into the next world, and remain so forever.

CHAPTER 9

The Separation

BECAUSE OF COUNTLESS DOCUMENTED ACCOUNTS, too similar to be coincidental, the *separation* is almost common knowledge today. Most of us know the scenario. Revived from near death, a person recalls having journeyed through a tunnel, observed a brilliant white light, and then a spiritual guide that the person often considers was a former loved one, a saint, Jesus, or even God, which it follows out the tunnel and arrives in the spiritual world.

I theorize that such guides are departed souls who sometimes tell the person to "Go back," if it's not their time to pass on. Other similar patients who seemingly journeyed deeper and returned, have even described reaching a beautiful, peaceful domain which they consider is heaven.

"Nothing follows death because when you're dead, you're dead," opponents, scientists, and others disagree, which could be the case. But if that were true, the same point would apply. The Creator would be superficial, and even stupid for creating both dimensions and us.

The so-called separation is the brain signaling the body to shut down the moment it anticipates the possibility of imminent death, they contend. *But this contradicts that many near/death patients survive the separation.* Also, if theory is correct, how come the mind chooses to give us the tunnel and white light images during supposed death but nothing for birth, unconsciousness, and other physical experiences? Also, were death final, wouldn't it be more logical for the mind to start experiencing nothingness or darkness during a near/death experience? The point is, the separation seems logical and brilliant, once again, something a loving Creator would incorporate into our scenario.

Whatever the case, upon death, even if we refuse to accept the separation's validity, having heard about it in this book or elsewhere, should enable even disbelievers to make the transition to the spiritual world, easier and hopefully without fear.

CHAPTER **10**

Grouping according to Compatibility

SOCIALIZING SINCE THE BEGINNING OF time, humans have instinctively congregated or grouped together with families, relatives, friends and others for companionship, help, education, and other reasons, throughout the world, even in primitive cultures.

In America we join the Knights of Columbus, Elks Club, Country Club, and others, plus organizations and political groups. Generally speaking, most of us avoid negative groups, such as certain cults, gangs, criminals, or the deranged, because, to repeat, most of us tend to be positive.

During physical life, we're fortunate if we have one or two close friends with whom we've bonded, need, or hold dear for various reasons, plus the usual peripheral friends, acquaintances, distant relatives, business people, and similar others. Some humans are prejudice against those belonging to a different race or who have different skin color, as we know, which is immoral and another negative attitude to avoid, especially since such characteristics are non-existent in the spiritual world.

Helpless during our very early years, we have no other choice but to depend on parents or others for food and shelter. Because they support us as we grow older, we frequently have to tolerate their attitudes, behavior, and values, et cetera, also true about what we learn in school. In other words, we're really brainwashed during these years, which could be positive or negative depending on many factors.

Parents and family members who are loving, uphold moral values, and teach us to be open-minded, self reliant, and kind to others, et cetera, is positive. Criticizing them for making us follow *their* religion which we later find faulty and reject for whatever reason (true in my case), is unfair. The point is, unless one is highly rebellious, a strong individualist, profoundly intelligent, and so on, each of us usually follows (or is brainwashed into accepting) the philosophy and precepts of its own generation.

The scenario is different in the spiritual world. Many revived near/death patients report that souls of departed family members and others greeted them, happily, like we often do here, following a long separation, which sounds logical. Arriving there after death, we would most likely reciprocate, although probably not if we didn't get along with them during physical life.

The point is, once there, we're really free. We're not obligated to associate with our parents, fellow workers or business people, former neighbors, and so on, but, rather, with whom we're most compatible. Furthermore, social status, education, awards, or similar concepts associated with the physical world, are irrelevant, there. Nor is a soul deliberately placed on a higher or lower level according to its moral advancement, which would be immoral for suggesting interference and favoritism.

CHAPTER **11**

Heavenly Music

MANY REVIVED PATIENTS DESCRIBE HAVING heard what they call "heavenly" music, that is, classical. This sounds logical, since classical music has "stood the test of time" for centuries. Apparently, the combined thought energy from billions of souls that reside there, sustain it, because classical music is superior to all other types for many reasons.

Critics might argue that such near/death patients *imagined* hearing heavenly music, but, if so, none that I read claimed to have *imagined* hearing rock, pop, or jazz, cetera.

Despite one's taste in music—and present world taste is poor at best—it is usually serious, passionate, and seems to embody much of the human spirit. Even its lightheartedness is superior to the best in popular music and other types, which songwriters gear to the commercial market.

The other types start sliding downhill in quality from there, particularly rock which is often simple, simply loud, sexual, and superficial. Many such rock songs often consist of no more than four chords, which, musically speaking, is like a child's limited vocabulary, and suggests immaturity. Lyrics repeated continuously are boring, and implies that such lyricist are equally immature and sell their souls to the commercial market and the masses for money, or they're simply untalented.

Unfortunately, because of their need to follow and "belong," many youths do likewise, that is, they sell their souls to whatever their peers' taste or whatever is the trend.

Though most jazz pianist like myself appreciate a rhythm background, rock drummers bashing romantic love ballads with sledge-hammer intensity, is tasteless and hardly communicates the sensitivity, warmth, and spirituality that such ballads require, especially considering that rhythm isn't music. Nor can I understand how some people claim to like *all* kinds of music. Some food simply tastes terrible.

Though improvising is difficult to master, many jazz musicians consider rock musicians' brand, feeble, immature, and corny—silly—suggesting that they never practiced the grueling rudiments. In fact, many rock musicians buy a guitar or drum and practice during rehearsals or even while recording.

African Americans created jazz, which I consider the second best type, because improvising well requires mastering the instrument and creating something new, original, and unique, without deviating from the song's chord and measure pattern, which is difficult, since this also requires great skill, intelligence, and concentration. The difference between the two types of music is that classical musicians play precisely what someone spent considerable time composing, whereas jazz musicians play (improvise) their own melodic line, which they compose immediately.

Furthermore, whereas rock musicians play mechanically, good jazz musicians often play from the heart, and their playing is often soulful, especially when performing love ballads. Those who disagree, have no ear for music, never studied the different types, or blindly follow the masses. Had many public school districts not dropped "music appreciation" from their curriculum, maybe American taste wouldn't be so poor in general, and we would probably reject so much junk music.

I rank country music third because, although simple, it often deals with the heart, is sincere, and depicts the average man and woman.

Since improvising is reflective and therefore spiritual in nature, once in heaven, as a former jazz pianist, I envision being able to think ideas into reality, which other souls might be able to comprehend, that is, hear. I also won't have to worry about maintaining rhythm or a certain level of technique (which thinking can create into reality, there), clunky, out-of-tune pianos, noisy, uninterested listeners, and tilters spilling drinks on me and the piano. I'll also be able to avoid unfair employers who rarely pay jazzmen what they're worth or they hire pianists like me to play background music as long as we don't play too loudly. (Also, I won't have to worry about paying bills or having enough money for food, shelter and the basic needs, which has haunted me throughout my life.)

Companies and others throughout America often select unbelievably atrocious music that callers, left on hold, are forced to absorb. Such music frequently consists of stupid, immature, two or four bar ditties, which, repeated continuously, punish the ear. Those responsible for selecting such crap, ought to listen to "heavenly" classical music which my publishing company, Balboa Press, offers, and even varies with different selections. Nor am I trying to patronize them in any way.

CHAPTER **12**

Grouping Together in the Next World and Miracles

WHATEVER WE HAVE BECOME AT death—the sum of our emotional and intellectual souls—we take to the next world, along with our baggage, good or bad. Nor can flipping a switch eliminate regrets, fixations, and so many other mental aberrations including strange habits, false values, and superstitions, which prevent us from advancing, morally, and grouping with more advanced, loving souls there.

Precisely what group each of us will join after death depends on which we find most compatible with ourselves and other reasons. Souls who followed particular religions here, will probably group with similar souls there. Souls that associated with Jesus, his parents, the Apostles, saints, and possibly the better popes will probably group together. (However, since popes have always lived luxuriously including even today, while preaching that we should help the poor, suggests that they are more compatible with hypocrites and the selfish.)

I speculate that the energy from the Jesus group or a similar Christian group was sufficient to cause the Fatama miracle and others but not enough to create our universe. During that miracle, mass hallucination obviously caused what appeared to be a jostling sun. But had that really occurred, Earth would have suffered catastrophic damage and been pushed out of orbit, annihilating civilization. Whether the three girls heard is difficult to determine and almost immaterial. More important is that if the reason for the miracle (and supposed others like idols of St. Mary weeping real tears), was to unite Christians and give them hope and faith in the Jesus agenda and Christianity, it has been successful.

CHAPTER 13

Idiosyncrasies of the Spiritual Dimension and Hell

REVIVED FROM NEAR/DEATH, SOME PATIENTS claim to have glimpsed cities like Tokyo, London, and New York on the other side, which they considered more beautiful and more majestic than those here. This seems logical since souls already there, would have *thought them into existence* in their purest state, that is, minus traffic jams smog, noise, and other undesirable problems such as darkness, which has no value. Such souls might even reside inside these buildings, including apartments, town halls, and homes, et cetera, like we do here.

Such *spiritual* buildings would remain until their supporting energy wanes or ceases for whatever reason, which is true, here. Sports arenas, buildings, ancient temples, for example, remain until we remove them or they decay on their own.

In his book, *Reflections on Life after Death*, Dr. Moody described having out of the body experience naturally, without suffering from near death. On several occasions, he managed to enter the spiritual world, and his descriptions of similar spiritual cities seem consistent with the near/death patients' reports just cited. Critics considered him insane, whereas we should be indebted to him for having the courage to reveal such important, controversial information.

If all this sounds implausible or far-fetched, most important to understand is that souls in heaven were previously in physical bodies like we are now, and we carry thoughts, aspirations, concepts, and so much more into the next dimension, why both dimensions would have some similarities.

Other near-death survivors claim to have observed areas (which I call *cells* for lack of a better word) containing fire, brimstone, flaming pits, raging infernos, and the like, which resemble our conception of hell, where souls called Satan, Lucifer, or the devil exist. (We still haven't decided who is running which inferno.) Nor would God have created hell, which would have been immoral. *We* imagined such souls into existence, and the energy from Satanic and similar cults sustains them here *and* there. Had none of us known or heard about them or hell throughout history, neither would probably exist.

Those who use the Ouija board, conduct séances, or perform related rituals, are sometimes amazed when doors supposedly slam by themselves, or when odd noises occur, and whatnot which they attribute to Satan and/or other negative entities. But if true, how can we compare such worthlessness to a power and energy that created the universe and spiritual world which It is holding together?

The souls of Hitler, Stalin and similar others probably reside together there with equally compatible others. Unless they change their attitudes before death, believers and supports of their teachings will probably join them after arriving there.

One difference between the two dimensions is that we use legs and other means for transportation here, whereas there, thinking where to go sends souls there instantly. In fact, souls there, must surely appreciate not having to transport themselves in such objects as cars, planes, and ships, et cetera, that wear out, break down, need refueling, and often kill us directly or indirectly with their toxic emissions.

Here, we instinctively *think* ourselves away from noticeable dangers such as flooded roads, wildfires, and landslides, et cetera, and the body complies, which is true there. Frightened after viewing hell, for example, the curious are capable of willing (thinking) themselves away instantaneously.

Murderers, rapists, and so on, who believe (*think*) that they should reside in hell as punishment in order to atone for past sins or for whatever reason, will send themselves there. Such souls will then suffer mentally, that is, spiritually (which is more painful than physical), according to how much they *think* they should, to what degree, and how long, which could be forever.

Whatever the case, whether we're here or there, *we* chose where and when we wish to transport ourselves, not God. Since we carry our thoughts to the next world, jokingly wishing someone to "Go to hell" for whatever reason, is unwise, or at least unkind.

Former family members and spiritual guides probably help incoming souls overcome their past evil deeds, including even murders and rapists, if they are sincerely regretful and repentant, but probably not history's worst offenders like Hitler, Stalin and the rest who most likely will reside forever with other compatible negative souls.

CHAPTER **14**

More about How Thinking
Creates things in the Spiritual World

BECAUSE MANY SOULS HAVE PASSED into heaven over the centuries (and cost isn't an interfering factor like here, they surely have *thought* into existence the most beautiful trees, shrubbery, and flowers rather than the less desirable, the poorly formed or the diseased).

Roses and peonies, for example, probably grow unbelievably large, colorful, and exquisite, or they might simply exist, rather than grow, true about beautiful birds flying about for earthly realism and esthetic value, again depending on the thinking (thought energy) that created them and continues to sustain them.

If bees are included, surely souls would have enough sense (love) to exclude stinging which has no value. (Besides, physical pain is an earthly concept that we will either learn to exclude from our thinking, or it will simply disappear automatically, since we will lack bodies once we're there.)

Since many of us enjoy playing golf, links and similar spiritual areas would probably abound there in spiritual form also, but, again, in their best, purest state, without noisy planes, insects, bad weather, and other physical annoyances, including unruly spectators.

Speculating how souls would play or compete with one another, is difficult. A soul teeing off could *think* the ball into a hole, for example, while other souls could try to direct it into the rough. Where the ball lands could depend on how much combined thought energy superseded all others and directed it there, and so on.

Possibilities abound, which I leave to the reader's imagination. Once in the spiritual world, since I don't play golf, I probably wouldn't visit that area, except, perhaps, out of curiosity.

Here, we speak through voice boxes (which we cannot do there, without a body, of course) or we use the air waves and contraptions called phones that amplify our voices through wires we string along poles or underground. There, souls, communicate, telepathically. Nor can we disguise lying or deception, since telepathy allows souls to read one another's thoughts instantly.

Though hunger isn't necessary, a soul recalling or thinking about that physical condition, could experience it there. If it recalls a steak on a plate on a table it remembers during physical life, all will appear, including the spiritual fork and knife, which is all invisible to us residing in another dimension. Imagining eating the steak, a soul could experience familiar thoughts like taste, swallowing, and enjoyment, if that soul *thinks* it should. The intensity or contentment would depend on what the soul recalled during physical life. A soul could even produce any negativism associated with eating, such as stomach pains, indigestion, heartburn, and so on. Eventually, unless such a soul is obsessed with eating, which has little value there, it would most likely reject thinking about such a physical concept, particularly if it had indigestion problems.

Whether we're here or there, the essence of us, our souls, control what we wish to remember concerning physical life, how much, how long, and to what extent. The main difference between the two dimensions is that thoughts have more immediate power there than here.

CHAPTER **15**

Receiving Energy from Souls on the Other Side?

THOSE STILL CONNIVING, LYING, CHEATING, seeking revenge; those without remorse for having hurt others, deliberately or unintentionally; those who *aren't* striving to overcome such fundamental flaws and become morally good and loving, won't attract the proper energy from the more advanced souls in the next world.

How loving, good, and spiritual one is during physical life, affects the quality and degree of energy received from similar souls, there. "Like attracts like" in both dimensions. Here, kind folks attract the same, and the mean, the opposite. Though the mean sometimes take advantage of the kind, ironically, they're much better off than the mean who have much more to learn and reject. In other words, it's better to be kind and suffer because of the mean, than mean, which is a major, negative flaw that's difficult to overcome in the next world.

Furthermore, since the material world is the learning plane, we learn from suffering. Had we been born compassionate and loving, we wouldn't learn about such negative concepts as lying, starving, and killing, et cetera, which, in a sense, is also unfortunate, but that was (is) the scenario that God created for us. Because of world misery, cruelty, man's inhumanity towards man, and so on (including one's own suffering), many good souls despair, which is unfortunate. Some even regret having been being born, but they have no choice, and I sympathize with them. Nor is it easy to accept that we learn through suffering, probably more than those who live happy lives and never suffer. Suicide is a terrible option, and such near/death survivors report that good souls there criticized them for such attempts.

Those who doubt that we can communicate with good souls and/or their energy in the next world, close that door, comparable to rejecting the concept of a telephone which would negate answering it if it rang.

Accepting the possibility that physical life is the learning plane which precedes the next dimension, which I consider the real world, and enlisting help and guidance from souls already there, is easy. One need only ask (pray) for their help while meditating. Whether or not one will receive it often depends on the request, why, and countless other reasons.

Ironically, such praying frequently sets *us* up to focus on our problems and for *us* to solve them, not souls in the next world. If we chose to ask a particular soul for guidance such as relatives there, so-called saints, Jesus, or The Father, et cetera, I theorize that such souls are capable of responding in some way, if the situation is right. For example, help or guidance might arrive as a sudden insight or solution to a problem, which many have experienced, as I have while writing this book. Guidance could occur during a strong urge to open a certain door, figuratively speaking, while avoiding or closing another.

A sudden impulse to drive a different way to work or wherever, could be attributable to spiritual guidance helping us avoid an accident and possible injuries, which wouldn't have taught us anything. Afterwards, having learned about the rock slide or sudden flood that awaited us, had we followed our original plan, often surprises us. Death would have ended our chance to learn new, meaningful lessons or change old ones. How we are destined to affect others, to what extent, and how long, for example, might be another reason why we manage to escape death when we do.

Spiritual guides or other advanced souls, often one and the same, appear to be trying to guide us into "doing the right thing," that which is positive and loving. Some of us have even eye-witnessed seeing them in the physical world which they called *angels*. Since believers tend to believe and doubters tend to doubt, because I personally have never seen one doesn't negate their existence.

I feel guided. Despite my poor choices concerning money, desperately needing it to prevent economic disaster early in my first marriage, I was often surprised when I managed to acquire it from the most unlikely source, almost the precise amount, as if I weren't entitled to more. Coincidence, skeptics will disagree again. Though the burden of proof lies with those who believe similarly, can *they* prove that such moments *are* coincidental?

Incidents often occur or not for good reason, which reminds me about a car accident I had in my youth. Though the insurance company agreed on the repair estimate and sent me a check, I took a friend's advice, had the work done elsewhere for hundreds less and used the money to pay desperately overdue bills. Who can accurately determine if the friend received guidance to help me or was I steered to him for *his* help?

Doubters need proof, which is difficult to obtain in either or both possibilities. (Since then, most insurance companies have *learned* to write out checks to the repair shop, rather than the insured motorist. The few that haven't, don't care—quite nice of them, I thought then.

I make less bad major decisions today. True, I'm older and perhaps wiser. But considering occasions when I think I erred, they often prove to be correct in the long view, or, such decisions helped me learn something new or reject something detrimental.

The point is, guidance, help, or protection, seldom explodes at us in large doses, but, rather, often appears infinitesimally and/or unnoticed. The following simple anecdote illustrates how this might happen. Shortly before I finished writing my first version of this book, I bought a second-hand luggage carrier for my car for a planned trip. Brackets to attach it to the car's two top rails were either outrageously expensive or seemingly unavailable. Three parts stores didn't carry them, I soon learned. The salesman in the fourth store, thought he did, but, thumbing through a thick parts book, couldn't find the listing.

I was about to give up when his telephone rang. He greeted his friend, another salesman at a similar chain store, eventually asked him if he knew the whereabouts of the part in the book, which he did. Coincidental? or was this spiritual help? I could only wonder. Whatever the case, in order to help us understand the nature of guidance and energy we seem to receive from souls in the next world, we should pay attention to such supposedly insignificant incidents and not attribute them to God's intervention.

To help others recover from severe injuries, especially incurable diseases, many of us direct rote prayers to God. Speaking naturally to souls in the next world, rather than the Creator, might not change matters, not because we weren't able to connect with them or they refused for any of many possible reasons, but because of what we need to learn or reject if and when the person continues to suffer and passes on. Objective analysis frequently reveals that the death of a close one was the right time considering how it affected relatives and others, true about myself after my second wife also died of cancer. Communicating with other souls can be accomplished anywhere, anytime, through meditating in a quiet room, verbalizing softy (without chanting) or simple thinking, namely sending out different, heartfelt thoughts without picturing or wondering who is listening. Sometimes I do so while driving.

Obtaining that Mercedes or mansion, or achieving sudden success in business, and so on, might suggest to some that God answered their prayers, when, in fact, their own obsessive focusing toward achieving such ends did. Nor would the more advanced, loving souls in heaven have been responsible, since they would be (are) inclined to inspire (help) those involved with worthy, benevolent matters.

CHAPTER **16**

Jesus

ALTHOUGH THE SUPREME BEING IS supposed to know everything, It cannot know what our choices will be until we make them. Also, if It *really* knew that we were destined to destroy ourselves, It wouldn't have created us. Though unaware of it, *we* are choosing to prevail or self-destruct, not God.

Because of so much violence through warfare since our beginning, especially during Roman times, I theorize that the Creator logically sent us Jesus, as a messiah, in order to teach us to love one another (and other reasons). But in our warped enthusiasm to uphold his teachings, considering the slaughtering that followed during the Crusades and other wars, this apparently backfired, which was *our* fault.

Yet, following his teachings over the centuries has probably saved many more lives than such losses, true about religions whose leaders preach that hell awaits those who disobey the Fifth Commandment, that *Thou Shalt not Kill*.

Whether or not Mary was a virgin is immaterial, especially since this cannot be proven or disproven. Nor could a God that created the universe and heaven have been incapable of accomplishing such a feat. The point is that this controversy, involving Mary, the Father, the Holy Ghost, plus scientists and others believing (having faith) or disbelieving in all this, was (is) brilliant for attracting world attention to Christianity's cause, once again, up to and including today. Furthermore, all this sets Jesus apart from Buddha, the prophet Mohammed, and others who didn't perform miracles, nor were they associated with them, true about magicians who preached fraudulently then (some even claiming to be messiahs), and others who suffered on the cross and maintained that they too had performed miracles (probably in order to save themselves from death).

Though Christ must dislike statues of himself strewn about in the physical world (which contradicts the Commandments), millions outpouring love energy to him through prayers and repeating his name, plus words printed on signs on car bumpers, in homes, and so on, throughout the world for decades, have most likely enriched or empowered the essence of him—his soul, that is, deepened the love energy that he possessed after returning to heaven, (for the lack of any other way to express this.)

True or not, I accept that he was morally perfect, cured the sick (including the lepers), and turned water into wine, et cetera. His rise from the dead, the disappearance of his body, and so on, is logical for symbolizing that all of us will follow suit. So are his teachings, particularly that we should love one another, et cetera, not kill off the species, which is especially valid and logical.

Though I can remember years ago asking God to provide me and my family with money for survival, and receiving it, as previously cited, I despised money and all that it represented (possibly because I was always broke), although, perhaps, mostly because I was (and still am), deeply spiritual, rather than materialistic, and/or money-hungry.

Throughout my life, like many Christians, I asked Jesus and the Father to eliminate war and the suffering from famine and sickness. I also prayed for them to help others, be with me, and give me strength, et cetera.

On different occasions, I recall frequently asking Jesus to help me find badly-needed, misplaced tools, or help me locate a school when I was substituting, in order to avoid arriving late. Since I was always successful, I always wondered, was all this coincidental, or were my prayers *really* answered, until the following incredible incident settled the question, which occurred shortly before this book went to print.

In fact, I delayed having it published in order to recount it. Still broke and with a debt settlement company, I agreed to stop using my credit card to pay for anything. Two days remained in the year, and I didn't have a usual New Year's Eve playing job while visiting my girlfriend in Oklahoma City. I still needed considerable money to defray book publishing expenses, and prayed to Jesus to help me find a New Year's job, which was always more lucrative than the usual Saturday night gig.

Although my girlfriend suffers from osteoporosis and has trouble walking, the next day, we spent considerable time shopping in a health food store which was crowded because of the holidays. Though extra walking would aggravate her condition, because of expectant company, she insisted that we finish shopping at another store for some badly needed basics. Arriving, I noticed that the parking lot was full, except for the handicapped space closest to the front door. That's a break, I thought.

Driving there, I paused to allow a man to walk past who happened to be the chef who hired me to play at a restaurant two years ago.

We exchanged greetings and the following conversation unfolded, which I will repeat almost verbatim:

"Are you playing New Year's Eve?" he inquired, surprising me.

"No."

"How about playing for me at the same restaurant?"

Unbelievable, I suppressed. The chance of running into him in such a big City, precisely at this moment, *has* to be astronomical, flashed a thought, while I agreed to the terms, and we eventually parted. "That's exactly what I had prayed to Jesus for last night," I told my girlfriend while parking.

"Guess what," she announced, equally as spiritual as I and also a believer. "Before we arrived, I prayed to Jesus asking for that particular space to be available."

One incident could be written off as coincidental, *not two*, I emphasized while we entered the store, and she agreed.

CHAPTER **17**

Generosity Versus Selfishness

THE QUESTION ARISES, WHERE DOES the need for comfort leave off and selfishness or greed begin? which each of us needs to answer since it affects our souls. Naturally, this is immaterial to atheists and others who disbelieve in God or an afterlife, which, incidentally, can cause some disbelievers to be ruthless, unforgiving, selfish and materialistic or simply hateful and evil. On the other hand, trying to convince disbelievers through this book that life exists beyond death, could coax them into striving to be positive and loving.

The world owes much to the philanthropic rich who have helped the needy throughout history. But many of the rich are stingy—why they became rich, some say, which isn't necessarily so.

Generosity, rather than stinginess, suggests a loving soul. Distinguishing between both is important because they're spiritual in nature, that is, they refer to our spiritual aspect—our souls, which connect us to the spiritual world. Nor can we learn to be generous in the spiritual dimension where nothing tangible exists.

Determining what we need for comfortable living before donating the excess to others, is relative to many factors that we need to analyze carefully while we're here, not when we're there when it's too late. This is why we often remind one another, "You can't take it with you." Ironically, anticipating death, many disbelievers who refuse to accept an afterlife, often go berserk, selfishly trying to spend all their money on themselves.

Oftentimes, our conscious—again, the spiritual aspect of ourselves—tells us whether or not we've been generous in certain situations. Donating a million dollars sounds generous but not necessarily, if the donor has ten million, if the money was simply a write-off, or if it went to an unworthy cause, and so on, which is sometimes difficult to determine. It also depends on how the nine million was used, such as for worthy, large scale projects such as building or rebuilding anything from a home to a shopping center, which the middle class or poor cannot afford to do.

A poor man donating his last dollar toward helping a destitute soul or toward a very worthy cause, is far more generous than someone donating a million from ten. So are those who deprive themselves, sacrifice, and even suffer to support the needy. The drunk, the derelict, and the vagabond who give up their cardboard beds for a newcomer, surpass all of us in generosity.

Nobody needs nine million to live comfortably, today. Though I realize that money earned from nationwide lottery goes to a worthy cause, I have always wondered why million dollar jackpots or more attract droves. Isn't a few million enough? Blessed are those who hope to win not just for themselves and family, but for the desperately needy.

I recognize that in a capitalistic society, were it not for rich business people who possess enormous capital to spend, we wouldn't have our malls, housing complexes, and much more. But if investing and reinvesting is only for the sake of increasing one's portfolio, without concern for others, this is selfishness and greed.

During the 08 oil crisis, several oil company officials earned upwards of forty-five million for the year. Whether they realized it or not, they were blessed, just like I was (am) for having the talent to play piano professionally and eventually write this book, but I can only wonder how they handled their blessings. Nor am I singling them out since others earn astronomical incomes also.

Worse are the rich who feel superior to the middle class and poor. Those who pretend they don't and those who lack a natural compassion to help others because they don't *feel* it's their obligation, should do so, intellectually, like paying a bill. Happiness and satisfaction will usually follow.

Before the 08 election, I talked to a woman who criticized the welfare system. Most of us know the argument which I'll paraphrase: "My husband killed himself working all his life. Why should we help those who can work but don't because they're too lazy, fake sickness, and expect others to take care of them?"

Obviously, she typifies the negative, unloving soul. Unless she changes before death, she will take that anger and lack of compassion for others with her, and join equally compatible but negative souls in the next world.

I appreciate that her husband and others who work hard throughout their lives, but some people, especially the jobless who want to work, would give anything to be in that predicament. The point is, her complaint is familiar and relative. Was her husband killing himself out of greed or selfishness, in order to accumulate as much money as possible? Did he *have* to work that hard? Could he have chosen another profession or business? and so on. What about the working middle class and particularly the poor who need to work hard just to have the bare necessities? I wondered.

Since we're all imperfect, the best way to handle the lazy who refuse to work (who are often unmotivated or have psychological problems), and the usual takers (who have poor values), is not to punish, prejudge, or begrudge them, but to rehabilitate them, if possible, as we know, because we have no other choice (unless we chose to follow how Hitler handled this supposed problem).

Accommodating such individuals, taking care of them, and even sacrificing for them, has to be the *right* choice, because doing so is positive and loving, the kind of attitude all of us need to take to the next world. If they still seem to be negative, unloving, and ungrateful, if not even belligerent after receiving free help, that's unfortunate, but that's *their* choice, which *they* will take to the next world.

Considering this differently, since most of us like to prosper, unless we're mentally sick, incapacitated, or have other problems, such individuals would have done so, had they been able, but obviously weren't because they didn't. The point is, all factors considered, such as genes, environment, influences, and whatnot, we can only function as best as we can at any moment in either domain.

Leaders of countries with rich oil deposits have the choice of being generous or selfish. They can help or hoard their resources, manipulate prices, and/or blackmail other nations, even poorer ones, et cetera. Many of them often chose the negative approach, meaning that after passing on, they will group with those who are as compatibly selfish as they. Arguing that they favor helping *their* people—those who happen to live on a particular section of the earth at a particular time, is prejudice and therefore immoral.

As humans, we are mostly in charge of what we can do or undo. Those responsible for allowing so many Americans to suffer from housing foreclosures during this time, will also need to answer to themselves. Once again, this was their opportunity (choice) to have true compassion for one another and back it up with sincere loving decisions, or not.

Luck, dishonesty, and ruthlessness sometimes enables the rich to amass great fortunes which, after death, they often will to greedy, unloving children who "blow it" on themselves. Rather than help the poor and destitute, others sometimes even will fortunes to animals, cemetery monuments, and edifices commemorating themselves and other absurdities.

Having experienced poverty, many of the poor and middle class are frequently more generous than the rich, particularly women rather than most men who are often too involved with their egos and power associated with money and their sex drive, to be as generous. Ironically, surrounded by such men, some career woman get trapped into behaving like men or feel obligated to do so in order to gain men's acceptance.

We're all familiar with the macho male who loves to unroll his roll before innocent eyes, especially those belonging to beautiful women. But I've never seen such greenery pop out of a woman's pocketbook. Most amazing is how so little is needed to help so many that have so much less.

Once again, the physical world is a stage that offers us the chance to choose between being generous and loving, or selfish, and our consciences, the spiritual aspect of us, helps us to decide.

Sometimes we catch ourselves missing the chance to help or tip someone. "I'll catch you later," we often say or "I'll lend you a hand," then don't, which is another example of lying.

When doubtful about tipping, for example, tip, if it's affordable, since jobs involving tips, usually suggest underpaid workers who depend on extra money to earn a decent salary.

While playing piano on the cruise ship, a doctor requested at least two dozen songs during two days. Though I played all I knew, he eyed the visible tip jar and left without feeding it. True, he might have lacked the cash both times. Returning to his cabin for a dollar or two would have been good for his soul, which probably needs overhauling. He also left me his card, told me to contact him if and when I'm in Florida. No way would I ever do so, unless he *really* needed my particular help for something. We're too incompatible.

True artists usually care more about losing themselves in their art, than slaving away to make money, why they're not too clever in business. Artists usually don't know how to invest, make the right connections or open the right doors at the right time, and so on. In a capitalistic society, determining what is a reasonable profit at another's expense, isn't easy. But salivating about monetary victories over others, suggests money-hungriness, which is an unwise attitude to take to the spiritual dimension.

Despite their faults, many religions teach us good morals, true about great spiritual leaders like Gandhi, Schweitzer, Jesus, and others. Sam Walmart, founder of Walmart was (is) a great soul. Nor is this an advertisement for Walmart. Many considered Sam Walmart stupid and irresponsible for giving away all his wealth and dying a pauper, when, in fact, he possessed love and compassion for others. Obviously, he sensed or knew beforehand, the true nature of physical life.

PART II

Autobiography

C H A P T E R **18**

Events in my Life that Led to the Paranormal

THE FOLLOWING CHAPTERS ARE AUTOBIOGRAPHICAL, including the supposed paranormal incidents that I experienced later in life, which should be possible for everyone to achieve, although under certain situations.

I respect those who believe in their religion, have faith that it is the ultimate truth, and certainly those who follow it, faithfully. As a Christian, I have always valued such concepts as *Give unto others as you would have them give unto you*, *It is better to give than to receive*, and so on.

I grew up in Brooklyn during the early Thirties, and at about age two or three, I can remember that everything in the physical world seemed strange: my bedroom, people talking, and vehicles passing noisily in the street. I also recall having trouble accepting that my awareness or the essence of me, that is, my soul was trapped into what I later realized was a body.

Although my mother was concerned because I was sickly, anemic, hardly ate, and rarely drank my milk then, she didn't know how to handle the problem or how to raise me or my sister. Often, she would angrily grab my ignored milk with one hand, one-arm me with the other, and sit me alongside my milk on the cellar landing leading downstairs into the dark, foreboding basement. "Don't call me until you finish drinking all your milk," she frequently shouted which she usually punctuated by slamming the door shut, which jolted me, and feverishly, or perhaps nervously, locked it, as if she were fearful that I would reopen it at age three.

Frightened about ghosts and snakes slithering up the stairs after me, I remember begging God to protect me and assumed *He* did, when they seemed to remain where they were, which I imagined was deep inside a sump at end of the cellar. Only after months of similar punishment did I figure out how to turn on the light above the landing, descend the open stairs (despite fears about a stray hand trying to grab me from underneath), and dump the milk in the cellar sink. (So, maybe God *did* help me, I sometimes reflect today, during seizures of superstition.)

During this time, I also found insects, animals, and plant life, unusual, which provoked my almost insatiable curiosity. Blessed with a basic love for living things, especially humans, I thought everyone felt similarly. Attending kindergarten, I soon learned otherwise. Most of the older males and even my own peers (not females), were unusually boisterous, unruly, and unkind. Often, they would rough up the smaller boys (or those who were unpopular, weak, and not as handsome as they, which included me). They also picked on girls, especially those who weren't as pretty and/or popular as others, and often kicked them during recess and after school, which surprised and puzzled me. I recall doing my best to protect such smaller boys and particularly the girls, including often retaliating similarly against the bullies, but that worsened the situation. Because I was skinny and not too strong, they frequently beat me up after school.

I particularly disliked that most teachers, who happened to be spinsters, had favorites, especially pretty girls and handsome boys. Nor was I one of them during my early school years, especially because, suffering from attention deficit disorder, unknown then, I constantly talked, couldn't sit still, and was unruly.

I also wondered what I was doing in the physical world, unaware that I had much to learn about life, particularly about this negative attitude in most males, that included ridiculing one another (especially me), which I also considered strange. Nor did anyone side with me against the bullies.

I was stunned upon learning that men actually killed one another, as depicted in the movies. In fact, misinterpreting everyone's optimism and patriotism when we entered World War II, I was so convinced that people didn't seem to mind, that I thought there was something wrong with me.

Growing up, I recall sensing my own kindness. I did my best to obey my parents, and was aware that although mischievous, I was really a so-called "good boy," for which I never received their praise which I desperately needed. I naturally followed their wishes and orders about how to behave and what religion to follow, as we do when we're young, because we have no other choice.

Since my parents constantly scolded us for tripping, banging into the wall, or spilling milk or water which never happened to them, I assumed that they were superior beings, like all adults. In fact, because I had so much trouble telling the truth, I thought that they never lied. This contributed to my feelings of inferiority, true about my sister who was loaded with complexes, especially because my mother constantly called her stupid in order to put some "brains in that numbskull," as she put it, which included hair-pulling, slaps, and whatnot.

Looking back, I know that my parents did the best they could. But blessed with intelligence and perception, I wondered why they couldn't correct us positively and lovingly how to sit, eat, or walk properly, and so on, nor did they ever praise us when we were successful, which is a negative way to raise children.

Accidentally breaking a dish or scratching a piece of furniture, frequently stimulated such an uproar, which often included reminders about our past wrongs and mistakes days and sometimes weeks before, that I soon understood why our neighbor's windows came crashing down, sometimes even a second time during such outbursts.

My mother scolded and ridiculed my sister so brutally for being slow, that she would eventually need psychiatric treatment. So would I, later on, particularly because my father, a successful musician, was constantly raging at me for acting up in class and that I was sloppy, clumsy, careless, and lazy, about everything, which, ironically, most young children are at that age. Nor was he aware how much he domineered and scolded me.

My mother began my Catholic indoctrination, which I consider brainwashing, at about age six. To please her and "get a better seat in heaven," as I heard my mother joke on one occasion, I began reciting countless silent prayers until I fell asleep, which seemed simple enough to please God, I reasoned. Convinced that God listened in and answered them, I was surprised when He forgot to tell Santa to give me a Lionel train set, one Christmas.

I also recall scolding Him, but quickly apologized, because I didn't want to hurt his feelings and secretly feared that He would send me to hell, if I didn't. Little did I know (until my father told me) that Santa agreed with God that I didn't deserve the train set because of my poor grades (though I was in an advanced class) and 'D's in conduct. I also noticed that my birthday presents began depreciating in value proportionally to my continued failure in both areas during those early years.

The first time my mother took me to church, I recall the priest's sermon about the importance of praying, and soon began increasing the number of "Our Fathers" and "Hail Mary's," I recited each night. In fact, as if praying were a game, I was constantly trying to break the record number I unleashed the night before, if I could only remember how many that was.

My mother revered my father because of his high income (He earned seventy-five dollars a week playing flute and saxophone on WOR in the morning during the early Thirties). Was this all there was to life? she nevertheless must have wondered, waiting on him, as he were a king, and she, his lowly servant and maid.

My father was also a professional egotist and Chauvinist, especially because he never stopped domineering my mother who lacked the patience to answer my questions about God, priests' angry sermons, and so on. "Ask your father," was one of her favorite lines, but he was rarely home. Renting a small studio in New York City, he was earning big bucks as a studio musician for NBC and CBS, and recording for such greats as Kostelanetz, Page, and Faith, quite an achievement for a man who had emigrated from Italy at age eight and had whistled through elementary school in a year and a half, which he continually reminded us at the dinner table. Nor did I remember to ask him such questions when he was home.

"You'll find out when you grow up," was another one of my mother's silencers.

Unaware about the importance of teaching us to be self-reliant, she felt obligated to do everything for us then—from tying our shoelaces to dressing us—which not only aggravated her, stressed her out, and made her unduly nervous and high strung, but also prevented us from puzzling out problems and thinking for ourselves.

Attending a novena with both parents for the first time, I eyed the priest at the altar and soon realized that his odd gesturing, incense snapping and loud chanting at a side room, wasn't directed at God (who I thought was answering with a loud, mysterious voice), but another priest in the shadows, which disappointed me. Nor did Jesus live inside the copper tabernacle on the altar.

Taught to believe that priests were "God's servants," and therefore superior to regular folks, I was surprised when they often took turns angrily berating Brooklynites for not contributing enough money for the new church addition.

Throughout my early grades, I secretly enjoyed acting up in class and being one of the class clowns, especially because I was better and wittier than the others. My clever imitations of newscasters and comedians, often broke up the class, which even included some of the most intelligent and prettiest girls, I was happy to notice.

Because our teachers were constantly belittling us with name-calling, including "stupid" and predictions that some of us were destined to land in prison (or hell), the class appreciated that I often imitated them behind their backs, which spurred me on.

Not until years later would I understand why they were also cranky, sarcastic and mean teaching the better classes like ours. Underpaid and struggling to survive until they could retire, teaching the many hoodlums in their poorer classes stressed them out.

Though my father wrote several stories and was somewhat talented as a writer, I probably inherited my music ability from my mother who had a nice voice and sang in tune. Although he could read and transpose music instantly, he had trouble improvising well, which prevented him from playing quality jazz, which requires, among other abilities, creativity and individuality, which he lacked. Like most staunch conservatives, he seemed to be overly cautious about experimenting or taking a chance, except in the stock market, and lost heavily, which he hid from my mother.

Painting for a hobby, he copied others, seemed to fear criticism, and often verbally maneuvered the family into praising him. He eventually painted originals, years later, which were stiff and uncreative, rather than passionate and bold.

Clearly, we were opposites, but since opposites often attract, we could have gotten along learning much from each other, true about conservatives and liberals. I needed his structure, confidence and encouragement, and he needed my open-mindedness, latent creativity, (and refusal to follow the norm) in his painting, writing, and desire to play jazz, which I could have taught him years later, since jazz is teachable, providing the learner is creative and has a good ear, et cetera.

Whenever I had problems trying to put together a model airplane or ship during those early years, he would criticized me, angrily, for not following directions or rules—which the true, creative artists often violates—and not doing things the *correct* way, which was often *his* way, and he was destined to disown me, much later in life, although for other reasons.

Looking back today, I realized that directions have been and still are atrocious, as if the writers are stupid, insane, or both. Recently starting to cook, I was appalled. Most authors have no concept about writing first things first, that is, putting things in the proper logical order. For example, I frequently had to reread recipes several times in order to prevent baking something before adding important ingredients, which would have ruined the food. How these books ever get published surprises me.

Computer directions are even worse. Concerning Windows Seven, headings such as *insert*, *review*, and *references* poorly describe what can be accessed. Reading *offline* initially, instead of the old-fashioned but precise *disconnected,* I thought my computer was out of line and considered trying to straighten it. Finding the alphabetizing icon is unbelievable *well hidden, well unidentified*, and microscopic, which is uncanny, considering that most companies need to alphabetize, including many of us. Concerning updates, we're ordered, "Please do not power off or unplug your machine," instead of the simpler, "Don't turn off your computer," and so on. Remarkable, how stupidity explains how to operate what genius creates. Nor is poor translating of foreign directions always responsible.

Customers trying to buy online are often offered inaccurate, wrong, or poor instructions how to order, what to check, or the box is difficult to find or even excluded, and so on, which is only a fraction of another endless list. One major problem is the inability of such authors to identify with average readers. Another problem is that the higher ups couldn't care less. Whatever they can get away with is fine. Besides, improving directions cost money and doing so would reduce profits.

Ironically, though, instead of hiring good writers to write clear, understandable directions about how to operate their gadgets, companies waste money hiring several people to do so over the phone, which is stupid. Customers put on hold are forced to listen to crap music and/or that they will answer in the order that we telephoned, which they repeat every twenty seconds or so, as if most of us are stupid, have short attention spans, or we're deaf.

Throughout my early life, though my father sometimes had the same problem understanding directions, I never heard anything like, "Yes, you're right, son. Sometimes directions are terrible," and therefore my feelings of inferiority sank deeper, despite sensing that I was intelligent.

My parents believed that money and material wealth superseded everything in life, which puzzled me because I was convinced that the opposite was true, and such brainwashing fueled my feelings of not belonging here and that I was really weird.

Also fanatically preoccupied with "keeping up with the Joneses," they never taught me not to lie, cheat, and steal, and much more, which I avoided mostly for fear of roasting in hell. Many traditional religions frighten us similarly, which is a negative approach, but, I suppose, better than nothing, since it helps minimize immorality.

My mother lived in a dream world. Possessing shallow values, she believed that the family was destined to become rich and famous. She also revered professionals, especially doctors, lawyers, movie stars, and political figures, in fact anyone well known, including gangsters, true about many of us today. Some women even write to such negative deadbeats serving terms in prison.

Coming from poor parents, she was also prejudiced against the poor. Her father was mostly an unemployed brick layer, and her mother worked in a sewing factory. My mother probably resented that her mother had her quit school and work in the same sweat shop as she, rather than any of her three other daughters.

Though this sounds conceited, my possible reason for having been born with such parents could have been in order to offer *them* a chance to grasp *my* insights, not vice versa. I sensed that they should have been more idealistic and romantic like me, not so materialistic, conservative, narrow-minded, and often cold, which I also didn't fully recognize until later in life.

CHAPTER **19**

Consequences of Horse-playing

I RARELY CAME STRAIGHT HOME after school during my early years. Possessing enormous energy, I usually rampaged through the vacant lots, up and down streets with my peers, which included the usual horse-playing and wrestling on lawns and angry window banging from home owners who even protected their dead blades in the winter.

Horsing around one day during fourth grade, I remember one boy who jump on my back and knocked me to the asphalt street. Though I reciprocated, he reached back, grabbed me by the collar, and pulled, and I landed face first on the asphalt, smashing my nose. Seeing stars, I rose shakily, and with blood streaming down my face, wobbled home without crying, because I wanted to be tough, I kept telling myself.

To avoid being scolded and lectured for never coming "straight" home during such situations, I always begged God to insure that my parents wouldn't be home, which I sandwiched between countless prayers. Finding them usually absent, as I did that day, I thanked God for answering my prayers. Shocked at the sight of me, my sister wiped away the blood and rinsed out my shirt, which I hung in the closet to dry.

That night at the table, my clever lying convinced my parents that I tripped over a curb while crossing the street, and I recall appreciating the usual lecture about my clumsiness and that I never watched where I was going. "Because you're always in a hurry about everything. That's why your marks are so terrible," my father usually shifted during such situations, and how he could always tie in my school work and D's in conduct, never stopped amazing me.

"My marks aren't so terrible," I once defended meekly, and the usual explosion followed, until I finally learned *not* to stand up for myself.

Checking the mirror the next day, I was upset upon noticing a bump midway up what was once a beautiful straight nose. Convinced that my father could do and undo anything, I mistakenly complained to him about it.

"What the hell do you think I can do? It's your own fault," I remember him storming and then somehow veering back to complaints about my 'D's in conduct, carelessness, and that I lost a Mickey Mouse wrist watch, which included Mom's support that I hung around with bums.

My classmates took one look at my nose and began uncorking "Eek, what a beak" or "Hello, banana nose, how's the weather up there?" and whatnot, which continued through the grades, particularly from my supposed best friend, the tall, handsome, Leo Amorosi, who usually wittily compared it to a periscope, an elephant's trunk, or the Washington monument, which stimulated the usual laughter from my peers, as we walked home from school.

I had befriended Leo mostly to please my mother. Thrilled that he was a doctor's son and had even invited me to his house, she always acted sickeningly pretentious whenever he visited me, unaware that he always reminded me that he was doing me a favor to do so, as if his rich, prominent parents had warned him against associating with such riffraff. Nor did I ever tell my mother who would have blamed me for treating him badly. In fact, I was always at fault whenever I complained about bullies or others.

"What did you do to make him beat you up?" she once asked when I revealed the truth. "Serves you right for hanging around with bums."

On one occasion when I criticized a teacher for being mean, I received such a bombardment from my parents, that I learned to keep such matters to myself.

Leo was proud of his oversized Lionel trains which traveled along tracks cleverly supported against the walls throughout his parents' basement. The train even continued across a trestle bridge that connected to an impressive network on top of their Ping Pong table, all of which fascinated me, especially the engine which even tooted when Leo pressed a button on his large transformer.

Leo appreciated my company because I made him laugh, as he often said, which flattered me, despite sensing that he would have otherwise dropped me as supposed friend. Little did my mother also know that he often begged me to visit him and would "allow me" to run the train, as he would say, but only if I would agree to box with him. That is, so that he could use my head as a punching bag, which he didn't say either, which I also withheld from Mom.

Though Leo was a good twenty pounds heavier than I, six inches taller, stronger, and possessed longer arms than mine, my agility and quickness surprised him. But the more I managed to sneak in a good punch, the more he wanted to "go another round," which I found risky, especially because he was so much bigger than I, nor did I care for boxing anyway, and then came the bargain: I could work the trains if I spent equal time boxing.

I always consented, particularly when the class heartthrob and future valedictorian resorted to begging, which flattered me again, until one day he jolted me so hard in the head that I felt dizzy, and we stopped boxing.

Worried about the consequences (rather than if he had really hurt me), he begged me not to tell his mother (who was in the kitchen), which flattered me even further. Hardly the informing kind anyway, I promised I wouldn't and never did, because I already despised tattling (especially after learning about Judas), but I vowed never to box with him again, which I was destined to uphold (particularly after sensing the importance of keeping one's word), and left.

CHAPTER **20**

Analyzing the Church's Ritualism and
The Ten Commandments as a Young Teen

COLLECTION MONEY POURING NOISILY BEHIND the altar during mass, always jolted me. So did the loud organ music and a chorus full of older singers who seemed to be trying to out-sing one another, as if they were vying for the Met, that is, hoping to impress whatever Broadway scout might be attending mass, which surely amounted to zero, I suspected, but not my mother who never stopped fantasizing that my sister would be "discovered." because she also had a beautiful, mezzo soprano voice.

Comprehending the *Ten Commandments* for the first time, I was surprised. Making signs of the cross and praying to statues of saints and Jesus' family during "Stations of the Cross" contradicted the *Second Commandment* that we shouldn't worship idols.

How could soldiers be disobeying the *Fifth Commandment* and killing one another? I also wondered innocently, as Hitler continued rampaging throughout Europe.

The many different paintings of Christ disturbed me the most. Learning that he had died about two thousand years ago, how could anyone know what he looked like? I remember wondering. I asked my mother about it, but she didn't know either and also answered such questions with "Never mind" or "Stop fidgeting." Nor was Jesus born on Christmas Day, came another contradiction.

Though I appreciated the Christmas spirit and the toys I always received, I thought that people seemed more concerned about trying to outdo their neighbors with floodlighted ornaments and statues of reindeer, Santa Claus, and Christ, than *really* following Christ's teachings.

During seventh grade, we had permission to leave school early in order to attend a nearby church for religious instruction (that is, religious indoctrination). As usual, I always flew out of school with the others. In fact, my father was right. I was always in a hurry. Because horse-playing in the streets with my peers always followed, I was usually last to arrive at the church, and would bang on the locked door for admittance.

Father O'Glocklin, our catechism teacher, usually opened it, although not without unleashing a severe reprimand about my constant tardiness, until one day he had had enough. He raged open the door, swung and missed at my slanted head when I ducked, and this time my nose gave the concrete railing a good bashing. He ignored the blood squirting out of my nose, slammed the door in my face, and I trudged home. My sister was the only one home, and I thanked God for answering my prayers again. We went through the same routine as before, except, having learned that ice minimized swelling, I applied it, and was happy that I only suffered a slight disfiguration on my nose's left side, which my parents never noticed.

CHAPTER **21**

Prejudice in the Boy Scouts

I JOINED THE BOY SCOUTS that year. But because I had been getting D's in conduct throughout my elementary school, my father refused to send me to Ten Mile River Scout Camp for two weeks that summer, then changed his mind, which surprised me at first, until I realized that Mom had intervened in my behalf, and I thanked her almost tearfully. I was even happier upon learning that Frank Rizzo, my scout companion from Troop 194, would also be attending. My father arranged for us to travel together on the same train, and stay at the same cabin, which I appreciated.

In fact, looking back, I remember that except for abusing me with thunderous reprimands about my 'D's in conduct, sloppiness, and whatnot, he was usually in a playful mood, often took me fishing at Sheepshead Bay. He was always genuinely concerned when I was sick, often brought me pine nuts and candy as I struggled to recover, and so on, but nothing can erase mental abuse.

Arriving at the camp, we carried our duffle bags to the cabin, and I recall another surprise. My assistant patrol leader, Dave Troyanski, and another scout, Larry Feldman, both sixteen and Jews, were already inside, assigned to the same cabin.

Greeting us, both scouts simply mauled and battered us to the hardwood floor. At first, I thought they were joking, until they called us wop bastards, and ordered us to be their servants. This included making their beds daily, cleaning the room, and attending to their every needs, like picking up their mail and washing their clothes.

Speaking to each other or to them was forbidden, and they manhandled us when we did or slammed us into the wall lockers, which they were doing anyway.

Reporting all this to our scout leaders would result in an unmerciful pounding, they warned, and we never did. Nor did I tell my parents. In fact, shortly before the two weeks ended, ironically, despite the beatings, I enjoyed the surrounding country so much that I asked my father if I could stay another two weeks, which he denied because of my poor conduct and "lousy grades."

CHAPTER **22**

The Abusive Outside World

ONE DAY, DURING EIGHTH GRADE, Leo's excessive ridicule about my nose encouraged the others to follow suit, until *I* had had enough, this time and raged at them to stop, which was a mistake since my high-pitched voice had little power. Someone deliberately pushed me into Leo from behind, and that did it for him. I still vividly picture him handing his books and glasses to two willing classmates, as if they were his trainers.

Sensing a fight, a mostly male crowd gathered hungrily and started cheering him the moment he started swinging away. Reciprocating as much as possible but mostly hitting his fists or long arms, I ignored his stinging blasts at my face, one even reeling me. All I want is to catch him once, just once in that cocky face, I remember urging myself, thought I finally did but only caught his neck, which caused him to smile sarcastically, and I stopped fighting. So did he.

Exhausted but thinking I won, I was stunned when the others started shaking his hand, patting him on the back, and congratulating him. Staring in disbelief, I watched them walk away. Noticing someone deliberately kicking my books into the street was too much, and the tears flowed. Severely battered, my head felt like it was on fire, I suddenly realized. My ears stung and I tasted my own blood. Pulling myself together, I remember uttering one silent prayer after another, for what reason I'm not sure, except, perhaps, because fighting was a sin, according to Father O'Glocklin. Though groggy, I withdrew my handkerchief and with a trembling hand wiped the blood from my nose and battered face.

Managing to collect my books, I wobbled home, and the same scene unfolded, as if we were rehearsing the same part in a play. Stumbling into the house through the back door, I thanked God that only my sister was home, once again, and I recall appreciating her mouth opening and her gasp as she stared at me in stunned surprise. She helped me wash, and the ice pack followed, which minimized the swelling in my nose and cheekbones. Not until much later did my mother arrive home from grocery shopping (and gossiping with our next door neighbor), which I attributed to God answering my prayers, and I kept thanking Him repeatedly, while nervously explaining to Mom that I had stumbled in the lots.

More thanks followed as she began reprimanding me for venturing into such forbidden territory, plus more prayers of relief upon learning that my father was sleeping overnight in the City after having recorded all day for Andre Kostelanetz. More recording continued the next day and although he might have noticed my battered face when we ate dinner that night, except for a few smirks, a frown, and an odd nod, he seemed too stressed out and tired to check me out or unleash an explosion possibly because Mom kept bombarding both of us about it.

Six weeks before I graduated, the elderly, obnoxious and sarcastic Miss O'Melia, my eighth grade teacher, sat me alone in back, because of my terrible behavior. This was my chance to turn over a new leaf, I thought. Picturing receiving an 'A' in conduct, I resolved to sit still and not speak, whisper, or make faces, which I accomplished with great difficulty because of ADD and because my male peers, especially Leo, kept taunting, laughing, and jeering at me behind her back. Nor did she reprimand them in my behalf, when she caught them. Though such injustice stunned me, I visualized receiving the 'A' and held my tongue. For extra credit I even sat still with hands folded on the desk like a saint whenever we weren't reading or writing.

The six weeks finally ended. Miss O'Melia passed out the report cards. Overjoyed about finally getting an 'A' in conduct and pleasing my father, I opened the yellow card, and was stunned. Nor could blinking and frowning erase another 'D'. Dazed, I rose, feebly protested at her triumphant face smiling sarcastically, but to no avail. Nor do I remember descending the noisy steps filled with screams of happiness that the school year had finally ended. Convulsing while struggling to hold back tears, I crouched, dropped the card into the sewer, and vomited.

A car drove past without me hearing its motor, which I was destined to blame on poor hearing. Looking up, I was further jolted. Unaware that I had already begun drifting deeply into the safety of myself, I couldn't understand why the long row of houses on both sides of the school were retreating, that is, diminishing in size.

CHAPTER 23

Resuming the Piano after Flunking out of College

NOT UNTIL DAYS LATER DID I realize that I had graduated. Weeks after that, my parents sold our house, and we moved into a large, old house on Long Island.

I started high school, and continued upholding Christian values mostly because of so much local, gangland shootings, murder, and world evil, which included some maniac called Hitler. Besides, Jesus' life and death fascinated me, especially after learning that he never sinned, erred, and was morally perfect, whatever that was, I wondered then. I also learned that he supposedly cured the sick, and rose from the dead, which I thought was impossible.

How could they crucify such a wonderful, loving man? I also questioned, and was often moved to tears, especially because of my own suffering, none of which I revealed to anyone, much less my parents. Why didn't Pontius Pilate refuse to put him to death? I would have spared him, had I been Pontius, I also reflected innocently, and even pictured myself dying for Christ.

Though I praised God for being kind enough to allow a single confession to erase my sins, I was disturbed that visiting the confessing almost weekly wiped away my new peers' carousing, drinking, swearing, and fornicating. Though they were friendlier than those in Brooklyn and never ridiculed me about my nose (which wasn't as bad as I had imagined, particularly after I had gained weight), they often criticized me for refusing to attend their wild beer parties and general licentiousness, which annoyed me. Had the opportunity arisen, I might have attempted to have sexual relations with a willing female. But although sexual, I had too many problems, and wasn't too anxious to commit a moral sin.

Also, I was already so aloof and spiritual, that one day my mother asked me if I wanted to become a priest someday, which almost floored me considering my cheating and general lying. I even fantasized about having sex with girls and beautiful movie stars. Criticizing my mother (behind my father's back) about her materialistic ways and poor sense of values was also a sin, I suddenly realized.

"Er," I remember stalling. A *yes* was a *lie* which would offend God, and a *no* would do likewise for not wanting to serve him, I concluded. "I don't know," I uttered softly and sheepishly (hoping that God wouldn't hear). In fact, suddenly aware that my indecision was just as offensive, I almost choked.

Feeling guilty (and trying to make up with God), I started criticizing many of my peers for being hypocrites. Some laughed. Others considered me weird for complaining about their behavior, and I stopped, unaware how much I appreciated their friendship.

Priests constantly urging parishioners to give to the sick and poor, while the Vatican hoarded millions, bothered me even more, and I remember renouncing Catholicism then, but recognizing many of its truths, not Christianity, much less my love for Jesus or God. That my father had long since stopped attending church bolstered my decision.

But aware that I continued disrespecting my mother about her values, which I pretended to forget while still occasionally attending confession (to be on the safe side," I often thought), until one day, I recognized that I was just as hypocritical as they. In fact, I pictured myself following my father into hell after we passed on. Who knows, I might even get along with the old man down there, I thought with a laugh. Years later, like many others anticipating the end, my father was destined to rejoin the church, and give the beads a heavy workout.

I also wondered how hell could be somewhere deep in the earth, as I had heard during elementary school. How could they force you down there? I recollect asking my sister at that time.

"They just drag you down," she had answered, dropping my jaw.

Treating my male peers and others kindly and respectfully came easy and natural to me throughout high school. Why most of them couldn't reciprocate, bothered me enough to reinforce that there was something wrong with *me*, not them.

Although they appreciated my good sense of humor, they teased me about being different, which I tolerated. Nor did I want to be like them anyway, I often told myself, unaware that I was becoming an individualist.

Looking back, that moment seemed to arrive accidentally, one day after school. Several classmates offered me a cigarette, which I finally tried after some coaxing. Coughing, I told them that smoking was stupid. They laughed, ridiculed me, which I stomached, and I never tried smoking again.

My first experience concerning death occurred during my senior year. John was the only child of poor parents who were struggling to save up enough money to put him through college. I had barely befriended him when he passed on unexpectedly, which stunned me, particularly because he had won scholastic awards and honors in science, and was probably a genius.

Loving like his parents and possessing basic compassion for others like me, he was the only one to urge me to continue doing so, which strengthened me to believe that that I had the right attitude, not my parents who disagreed with helping anyone but themselves. Learning how my parents and others had treated me, he urged me to forgive all of them, which I couldn't do until years later.

John was also significant in inspiring me to strive to do my best at college and whatever I undertook, from how to sweep the floor, to how to build a house, especially since we're all endowed with that ability, he insisted, which I accepted and have followed to this day.

"Why be lazy, indifferent, and sloppy and strive for less when, as a human, you're far superior than the animals?" I often asked my unruly students when I eventually taught senior high school English.

"What difference does it make? What's the big deal? All we care about is bucks," my couldn't- care- less male wonders were destined to respond.

Today, I speculate that the big deal is that such unloving, negative souls will join and support similar negative souls in the spiritual world, which could have the negative consequences that I mentioned.

I graduated high school with about a "C" average," which was reasonable because of ADD and because I never opened a book, except to struggle to read and answer math problems.

Though I was unable to comprehend anything without my mind wandering, I applied for admission to Champlain College. They accepted me, and I flunked out in the spring of 1949 at age nineteen, which devastated me again. Feeling guilty about wasting my father's "good money," as Mom always said, I braced myself for his outrage, which I would have welcomed, but he hardly said a word, which surprised me. I guess he's happy about saving some heavy bucks, I concluded after recovering from the shock weeks later.

Despite our differences, my mother felt sorry for me, which I appreciated, and then came still another surprise. Using saved food money, she reinstated me that summer into summer school on probation behind my father's back. But lacking guidance, which I didn't know was available, I foolishly signed up for chemistry, which was doubly difficult, since I hadn't taken it in high school. Watching the professor write equations on the blackboard, I retreated so deeply inside myself that I barely heard his lectures and was completely lost. Also possessing a poor memory, I foolishly took physics, which I enjoyed in high school, and failed both courses.

Flunking out again with no chance for readmission, I was a study in gloom and negativity while hitchhiking home with two veterans on a cool, drizzling day. One of them asked to "borrow" my stylish Hawaiian shirt just because he liked it and wanted to "try it out," as he put it. More vulnerable than ever because of my mental state, but mostly because I believed in being kind towards others, I removed it from my back. Freezing in a t-shirt, I handed it to him, and he never returned it, which taught me another lesson about giving to others. I had to take care of myself before attempting to be generous toward others.

Eventually learning about my mother's generosity and compassion, my father said nothing, which shocked me even further. He's too involved making big bucks, or, maybe she's finally mellowed him, I recall thinking, unaware that his doctor had warned him that getting upset could lead to a heart attack. He even started exercising, which rattled me again, since he was hardly physical and disapproved that I had wrestled throughout high school, which took valuable time away from studying, he had always complained. Little did he know that I was barely able to read comic books in those days.

Because my mother longed to live on one floor, my father sold our house, bought an empty one acre plot across the street, and hired an Italian contractor to build a ranch on it. But he and my father ignored warnings from my uncle Joe, an engineer, who insisted that the foundation needed to be set higher above ground. Consequently, following its completion, water kept seeping in from the nearby sound during high tide which infuriated my father.

I sympathized with him, though we didn't get along, but was soon amazed. Not only did he refuse to blame the contractor because he was Italian, but he stubbornly refused to have him jack-hammer it out, despite complaining vehemently to my mother that he had been "taken." In fact, convinced that humans so tinted were superior to others, he hired another Italian contractor who wasn't much better.

Although he eventually built the foundation successfully (where my uncle had suggested), I noticed that the floor was unlevel in some areas and lacked certain promised designs, told my father, and he was stunned, especially because the problem couldn't be rectified.

Weeks later after we moved in, having long since recognized my own talent and that I had a good ear, I told my father that I wanted to resume taking piano lessons. "I'd like to play professionally," I recall adding almost timidly. Nor did I sense until years later that, were I to excel, I would be challenging him for the family's and our relative's attention, which he wouldn't appreciate, nor did his gloomy, negative doubts about my success surprise me.

"You can't stick to anything or finish anything," he unleashed at the dinner table where such matters were discussed and rehashed repeatedly, which invariably sent my stomach into churning, and he reminded me that I never completed jigsaw puzzles that I started or model airplanes.

Oh, God, not again, I recall complaining inwardly since I couldn't have been older than five or six back then.

"You can't even follow directions," he repeated, which included, this time, my failure to assemble toys during Christmas during those early years.

Neither can you, I finally recognized for the first time, but suppressed saying so, since I dared not challenge him about anything. In fact, I was afraid to speak up to anyone then.

Though I assured him that I loved the piano, he hammered away that earning good money as a pianist would be difficult because of the competition, "even when you're good," he emphasized with a touch of self-pity because he was still convinced that Jews were waiting in the wings to replace him.

"They're everywhere," he used to complain so frequently when I was very young, that I was constantly searching for them hiding behind trees or in the nearby vacant lots in Brooklyn.

"Piano players are a dime a dozen," he also added, which Mom seconded, as usual, and her patronization annoyed me because I knew she really didn't know.

Though she was usually fearful of disagreeing with him, she convinced him to pay for lessons, which would stop if I fooled around and didn't practice, he warned.

When's he going to stop treating me like a kid? I suppressed, appreciated another chance to prove myself, and thanked him almost tearfully.

But doubting that I could travel to the City on my own, which fueled my feelings of inferiority, he found Dr. Russell Farmington, a retired Julliard teacher from Queens who was willing to teach me at home.

My father was home when Russell arrived and rang the doorbell. Standing nearby, I watched my father open the door. Russell happened to be an African American and my father's jaw almost left for the floor. I guess Julliard never warned him,

I thought with a laugh as he pulled himself together and quickly overflowed him with hypocritical attention, which sickened me.

I began practicing between six and eight hours daily during the ensuing weeks, which hardly impressed my father who said nothing. Occasionally, he would enter the living room, suggest that I rephrase a classical passage or correct a missed accidental, even after I had done so because of my good ear. But numerous complexes including ADD prevented me from focusing and concentrating. High strung and nervous by now because I didn't know what else to pursue in life should I fail with the piano, I could never relax, especially when he was home. In fact, worried about getting pounced whenever I played a wrong note didn't help, nor could I retreat into what jazz musicians call "the zone," that is, deeply inside the self, which was saturated with doubts, insecurity, and guilt that he was still supporting me and even paying for the lessons. I wonder how many hours the old boy sweated out practicing in Italy as a kid, I criticized underground, during seizures of self-pity.

Sometimes, he would enter the living room with his alto sax. With loud bravado (so my mother and sister would hear), he would transpose a Bach Fugue or anything else instantly, which impressed me to the point of praising *him*, which he appeared to soak up proudly. Showoff, I eventually thought, unaware that I envied him.

"Do you think your father got where he is without practicing for hours?" Mom usually shouted from her hideout or prison—the kitchen.

Weeks later, I realized that Farmington wasn't teaching me anything that I couldn't learn on my own, except, perhaps, theory, which disinterested me because it consumed too much lesson time, nor was I planning to become an arranger, and told my father.

"Really," he responded, looking up from his desk.

Though he frowned, I sensed his surprise about my shaky attempt to assert myself without seeming ungrateful about spending his "hard-earned money for lessons," as he always said.

"You mean that you want me to look around for another teacher?" he needled as I stood with head down before him.

"A, yeah, if you could," I tried to say casually, since I disliked having to obligate him again. "I'd appreciate it."

"Don't say *yeah*. I keep telling you."

"Yes," I remember replying, almost breaking up because the *yes* answered both complaints, but because laughing had often been misinterpreted as disrespect, I caught myself in time.

"I'll see what I can do," he nevertheless replied.

Shortly afterwards, he found me an NBC pianist, who charged $7.50 per lesson, which was expensive then, but he too proved to be worthless. Sometimes he would hold his two year old daughter on his lap and baby-talk to her during the lesson, which I thought was incredibly rude and insulting.

One day, while I was struggling to play an original by Stan Kenton who was my idol, especially for being ahead of his times, my teacher rose from his seat and started rolling a ball back and forth with her on the floor, which stunned me. That's it, I thought, but once again was reluctant to tell my father and ask him to find someone else. Nor would he appreciate me criticizing an adult, I knew. The guy could be one of his friends, I mused with a laugh. That would be the day, I answered inwardly, especially because, despite his prejudice against Jews, he secretly respected them. Adults and Dad, be damned. This concerns my future, I concluded, and told him.

Looking up from the same desk, he gave me another curious look, as if he were as surprised as I about me asserting myself, and agreed. He eventually found me a fine classical pianist from the City who insisted that in order to advance I had to play with stiff fingers and loose wrists. Stunned because I would have to do boring finger exercises for six months, I was reluctant at first. But his warmhearted encouragement, which even included an affectionate hand on my shoulder convinced me, and I complied.

Weeks later, though my technique started to improve, I still had serious problems. Lacking self-confidence and possessing a short attention span prevented me from maintaining a strong beat, so vital when playing with groups, whether jazz or classical, and even when soloing.

Not until years later, did I realize that creativity and fanatical practicing wasn't enough. I could only succeed as a pianist and writer, after overcoming my serious psychological problems and ADD.

Unaware that the beating heart and walking enables all of us to have rhythm, I thought I lacked it, which worried me deeply. Also, though I managed to work part time for pocket money, I felt guilty that my father was paying for food, clothing, and even my music books.

Nevertheless pleased about my improved technique, I revealed the good news to my mother in the kitchen (although in my Dad's absence, since he would have uncorked something negative, about it.) But I also mistakenly complained to her about my struggle trying to learn so many different chords.

"See, I told you it wouldn't be easy," she reaffirmed as his negative counterpart, and, as usual, passed it on to Dad who poured out more negativity, about the difficulty I would encounter "making it in the outside world," and so on, which deepened my gloom, fears, and insecurity.

CHAPTER 24

Joining the Air Force,
Becoming a Father,
and Black-marketing

THE KOREAN WAR BROKE OUT in 1950, months later. Expecting the Army to draft me, I hoped to play in a dance band, and decided to join the Air Force since they offered enlistees a chance to choose what field to serve. Auditioning was necessary, I soon learned, contacted the band director at Mitchell Field, and arrived days later.

Though nervous, I appreciated that he happened to be a Black, possibly into jazz, I thought, and would therefore be more sensitive to my playing, than a stuffy, conservative White, and I was right. Though trembling through a reasonably soulful version of *Body and Soul,* I was elated when he praised me afterwards. He recommended in writing that I was good enough to play in a dance band, if I enlisted for four years, which I did, two weeks later. I eventually completed six weeks of basic training at Lackland Air

Force Base, San Antonio, and received my orders to join the band at Seneca Falls.

Arriving, I soon discovered that beginners and bad pianos were alike. Both make good jazz musicians sound bad, which they hardly appreciate. In fact, jazzmen often evaluate one another according to how well they play jazz, not their character and personality, true about me after I began rehearsing with the dance band.

Annoyed about my shaky rhythm and failure to sight read complicated jazz charts, several former "Big Band" professionals conspired behind my back, and persuaded the band director to have me transferred, I was shocked to learn, and had trouble nursing more wounded pride.

I received new orders to join the Air Force Band in Wiesbaden, Germany, in 1951. But after struggling to maintain a good beat and focus on reading similar, difficult, jazz originals, while playing in the dance band, I suffered the same fate. A similar clique urged Mr. Lockwood, our handsome band director, to replace me, and my depression deepened.

Though I appreciated being able to tour with Frank Sinatra, Rhonda Fleming, Tony Curtis, Janet Leigh, and Ava Gardner who arrived to perform for troops at the different bases throughout Europe during Christmas, I became the lamb duck pianist.

More humiliations followed. Mr. Lockwood tried me out as the cymbal player in the concert band, but because of my problems, I continually missed cues, crashed away at the wrong places, and he demoted me to being a runner, that is, delivering regulations and documents from one barracks to another.

Nevertheless, shortly afterwards, Tom Pomeroy, one of the dance band's bass players, appreciated my wit, humor, and warm, outgoing personality, rather than how I played, and befriended me. I learned that he was dating Elizabeth, who was a nice German girl. Because jobs were scarce, she and Trudi, her best friend, worked as maids for American enlisted men and their families.

Tom and Elizabeth arranged for Trudi and me to double date with them, but the war (and false propaganda) caused her to despise Americans, and she needed much more coaxing before finally agreeing.

Heedless and innocent, I secretly believed that having sex would minimize my depression and solve all my problems. Consequently, after double dating with them and several times alone with her, we had an affair, were careless and irresponsible about taking precautions, and she became pregnant.

Many servicemen in similar situations were abandoning such women and their children before returning to the States, which I rejected as being immoral, especially because Trudi was loving, mature, and hardly spoiled. Though unaware of true love, I proposed, and she accepted.

But because America was still punishing Germans for their atrocities and losing the war, many servicemen like me were the real losers. Because of the unsigned Treaty, according to regulations, we couldn't marry, until three months before our tour ended, and my misery deepened. Fathering an illegitimate child was still a major disgrace then, particularly for proud Germans, and I sympathized deeply for the humiliation and embarrassment I caused her.

Such injustice demoralizes the mal-adjusted more than normally, true about myself, especially upon learning that marriage would have entitled me to an extra $140 for Trudi and $100 for each dependent. Also, she would have had free PX and maternity privileges.

How would I be able to buy diapers, baby food, and other necessities for the child on a measly $110 per month as a PFC? I protested inwardly and ruled out revealing all to my parents, much less asking them for money, or Trudi's poor parents. Renting a partly bombed out flat, they had less than nothing, I knew.

Trudi continued working as a live-in maid for a staff sergeant and his family who lived, rent free, in a nice apartment which the Americans had confiscated as part of the war's reparations. Too bad I don't qualify for such luxury, I moaned inwardly. Considering my circumstances, I asked Mr. Lockwood if he could promote me to corporal, and he practically laughed me out of his office. I was in the wrong place at the wrong time, I recall reflecting painfully.

"He made his bed. Now he has to lie in it," he commented to the band behind my back during rehearsal one morning, which eventually trickled down to me.

True enough, I thought amid my gravity. Lost in self-pity, I arranged to have a mid-wife deliver the baby. Maybe I could somehow make corporal, if I improved my piano playing, I thought, and, whenever possible, buried myself inside one of the two small piano rooms in the large rehearsal room and practiced my scales and arpeggios with almost superhuman diligence and gusto, as if I were secretly trying to impress my father. Little did I know that I also needed to practice songs, that is, increase my meager repertoire.

"Rank's locked," Mr. Lockwood soon announced to the band, which was a lie, since promotions were occurring throughout the base.

Lockwood was in love with himself and couldn't care less about promoting anyone, the bandsmen realized.

"He's trying to save the government peanuts, so it looks good on his record," many of us concluded.

Suffering from narcissism, a phrase we eventually bestowed upon him, he often told the pretty *frauleins* who worked at the PX how handsome he was and that he was willing to date them, which they all ignored, we were happy to learn. During rehearsal, he also predicted that he would make colonel, which became a reality, years later.

Giving up about being promoted, I eventually asked him for advice and help about how I might circumvent regulations and get married. This time he promised to "look into it," which wasn't going to happen, because he's really a bull-shitter, like so many others, I finally understood.

Fanatic about impressing his superiors in order to advance himself, he was too preoccupied booking the dance band and concert band at every conceivable base throughout Europe, including the most remote Army bases, and the marching band suffered from having to drag their instruments and slosh through some of the worst mud holes and craters left over from the war.

"How come you guys bother playing in this God forsaken dump?" I recall one Army musician asking us while we were eating together in their mess hall after performing for them inside one of their tented barracks. "We got our own band."

"Thanks for telling us," I remember one of us responding. "We know where our leader's coming from, man."

Bypassing our worthless band director, I arranged to see one of the senior base commanders, a lieutenant colonel who counseled airmen like me. "Regulations are regulations. There's no way to override them," he commented in a phony condescendingly grave tone.

According to what I had heard, some airmen *did* manage to bypass them, I conveyed humbly, but it was no use. Amazing how many of us are capable of helping others or are in a position to do so, but don't. Because they don't have enough compassion for fellow earthlings, I philosophized, regretfully for the first time, and left.

The base Chaplin could only provide sympathetic, spiritual guidance and suggested that I ask for God's help. Sure, I thought sarcastically and eventually asked the Red Cross if *they* could help me.

Since a German national was involved, "Our hands are tied," a volunteer woman informed me, but was kind enough to give me some toothpaste and soap which, ironically, I desperately needed.

I wrote to my New York Senator who fed me the same unsigned Treaty line. Locating one of the airmen that had somehow overridden the regulation, I wrote to his senator, but he couldn't help either, because I wasn't a resident of his state, which depressed and upset me further.

The German Justice of the Peace agreed to marry us, but the Air Force wouldn't honor it. So, what's the sense? I reflected, and similar rejections continued for months. My only consolation was that my problems were miniscule compared to so much suffering throughout the world because of the War and many other reasons.

Trudi stopped working eight months later. Her parents lived about twenty kilometers away from the base, persuaded her to move in with them, and I insisted on paying them as much as I *couldn't* really afford for the rent, which they finally accepted reluctantly.

More bad news followed. According to regulations, airmen couldn't leave the base after hours without a pass, which most first sergeants throughout the squadron didn't always grant so easily, including ours who, ironically, happened to be hardnosed, and of German descent.

Because the military was trying to minimize the number of enlisted men returning late (or going AWOL) after beer-tilting or sleeping with poor and lonely widows and young *frauleins,* I anticipated having difficulty visiting Trudi. But rebellious anyway, especially about whatever I considered was unjust like my situation, lacking a pass wasn't going to stop me, I vowed.

Many stein-tilters and airmen in my situation felt similarly. Consequently, Friday evenings after hours, using tree limbs for support, we simply climbed over the fourteen foot, cyclone fence surrounding the base, and left for the night or weekend. Most of us, except those who went AWOL for a day or two, climbed back (including myself), and reappeared at their barracks for eight o'clock roll call and the usual announcements.

The Air Police either didn't know about our tree climbing, or did, but didn't care, until one day I remember them posting an AP who hid in the shadows behind a different tree some distance away from our favorite "maple tree with the shapely limbs," as I often joked to my cohorts, who simply eyed me curiously. No sense of humor, I labeled with a frown.

Catching us in the act, the young AP insisted that tree-climbing was against regulations. Appreciating such information, I considered throwing him a "thanks," but he seemed to be a likable guy from South Dakota, and I changed my mind. Separating after he left, the group found an equally accommodating maple, which we started using, and we were never bothered again.

Nevertheless, visiting Trudi presented another problem. Because the war had ravished the country so badly, trains and buses weren't running beyond city limits in 1952, and I would have to hitchhike. Though few Germans drove cars except mostly doctors and officials, I was surprised when sympathetic motorcyclists, particularly the youth, sometimes stopped to give me a lift, which helped restore my faith in human kindness. We could all *really* get along, if it wasn't for bad leaders, I also had enlightened myself.

Whenever I couldn't get a lift, which was mostly, I would walk to her house, stay until past two o'clock Monday morning, and walk back to the base, along a lonely, dark, deserted cobblestone road, without noticing a house for many kilometers. It's good for your soul, I recall telling myself.

Reaching Wiesbaden, I would sneak back toward the base along the debris-filled sidewalk, hide whenever I spotted AP's patrolling in jeeps in search of bandits without passes like me, and usually reached our barracks before eight o'clock roll call after climbing over the fence.

Except for some diehards, most musicians were hardly military-minded, particularly because of so many rules and regulations, and I appreciated that we had a common understanding. Whoever had guard duty in the barracks on Sunday nights, wouldn't turn in anyone who missed bed check and didn't have a weekend pass, which included many tree-climbing rebellious like me.

"If the Commies attack, it would be best for *regulars* like us," one of the bandsman began facetiously (while we played poker in the day room and drank good German beer, which was also strictly against regulations), "to lay down our horns and other shit, and surrender, man," he completed.

"We could serenade them with some jazz," another bandsman added in the day room, and although we laughed, most of us secretly feared that the Russians might cross the border and attack.

I'll never forget a young German named Hans. Wearing lederhosen and whistling, he would arrive punctually daily, on his bike shortly after the band finished rehearsing upstairs (and I returned from my deliveries), which he had timed perfectly. Nonchalantly, he would hop off and lean his bike against the high fence. From his wire basket, he would grab beer bottles that the bandsmen had ordered, and lob them over the fence to our waiting hands, which was strictly against American *and* German regulations.

Though we often missed some, we always paid him for everything, including the broken bottles, and sent him happily on his way to his next stop. This continued until the day a trumpet player named Duke simply cut a hole in the fence in order to save time and money, which the others appreciated, since I could barely afford buying necessities for Trudi, much less beer, which I hardly drank anyway, and we never got caught.

I soon concluded that black-marketing was my only possible hope of earning extra money to pay for the rent, the midwife, and so on. Because of rationing, servicemen were only entitled to buy a carton of cigarettes and a pound of coffee per week at the P X which profited us about $2.50 and $2.00 respectfully, on the black market, good money for servicemen then.

Resourceful out of necessity, I could make extra bucks paying bandsmen current black market prices for their rations which I could sell for more in the smaller, surrounding towns where the demand was greater, I realized, decided to buy a second hand car, which was cheap then, but nothing came easy.

Appreciating that my bank account was also in my father's name, I wrote and asked him to withdraw the $250 that I had banked from working at Jones Beach as a beachcomber during my senior year. But he refused at first. He questioned why I needed a car, claimed that I knew nothing about car engines, and reminded me that a local used car dealer had swindled me into buying a model-T Ford with a cracked block, years ago. Several exchanged letters later, he agreed reluctantly, and I bought a '37 Renault for about that price.

Trudi's parents were renting in a shabby, cramped three room apartment inside a large house. Built in 1640, it contained shrapnel holes from Allied bombing and strafing. Her mother cooked with wood on an old stove that heated the kitchen. Coal briquettes, dropped inside small, makeshift stoves, heated the small bedrooms. The outhouse, which they shared with other poor tenants, was located down a long, cold hall containing old, creaky floorboards. Unheated, it sported a leaky roof and warped siding which permitted snow to filter through, although only when it wasn't windy, which was never, I remember thinking with a laugh.

Talk about roughing it, I also reflected inhaling the usual aroma while seated on a rather clean throne notched out of a thick oak slab of wood. Dad should see me now, I often mused, recalling the times he called me spoiled.

During the weekends, I usually played chess with Trudi's father and her brothers, and struggled to converse with her relatives on Sundays, which helped me learn German. Brainwashed into believing that all Germans were cruel, I soon realized that most were simple, decent people who were struggling to survive.

(I also learned that, contrary to the American viewpoint then, most Germans that I met, including those in Trudi's family, were upset that the Nazis continued arresting Jews. Most refused to believe that the Nazis were exterminated them. Nor were they willing to discuss the matter for fear of getting arrested themselves and sent to concentration camps.)

Despite my learning problems, which I was beginning to sense, I knew that taking night courses for college credit would be relatively easy. Consequently, I took a six week course in conversational German from the University of Maryland, improved my speaking ability, and even received a 'C', which lifted my spirits, particularly since I had decided to return to college on the G. I. Bill. Maybe I'll be mature enough to make it through this time, I recall hoping.

One Sunday afternoon, I took Trudi on a pleasant drive throughout the picturesque Black Forest. We had dinner at a quaint German restaurant in Niedernhausen, about twenty kilometers from the base. I paid Josef, the owner, with a carton of cigarettes for dinner. We talked, and he agreed to buy large quantities of black market goods from me.

Days later, I started buying coffee and cigarettes from the bandsmen, most of which I sold to Josef, profiting about two marks or so per item. I even sold him soap and other items from the PX, which Germans couldn't afford or which weren't available on the open market. I profited about twenty dollars a trip, but without Trudi, who was afraid of getting caught and was also getting along in her pregnancy.

Most of Josef's small clientele consisted of senior citizens who were handicapped from having fought in the war. Ignoring my supposedly sly deliveries into the back room, they were surprisingly friendly and curious about meeting an odd, young American of Italian decent with dark black hair, and hazel eyes who was even a musician.

Josef occasionally treated me to a *snitzel* or *bratwurst*, which I enjoyed, although once I think he stole a carton of cigarettes and a pound of coffee, which I wisely ignored for fear of losing him as a good customer.

Sometimes some of the elderly Germans treated me to a huge stein of beer, insisted that I stay and drink with them, which I did several times, and I was surprised how well we got along. But though I enjoyed such great beer, I wasn't a drinker. I didn't want to feel obligated to treat them back, which I couldn't afford, and never stayed long.

Gasoline was expensive for Germans. Rationed for car-owning servicemen, which included low-ranked servicemen like me, we were allotted fifty gallons per month. Because the Renault got good gas mileage, I was able to sell the excess to a doctor that I met through Josef. The doctor even supplied me with five gallon canisters, and I was able to profit about four marks per canister whenever I delivered my laundry bag of goods to Josef.

Most of us disliked Sergeant Carl, our first sergeant. A staunch military man, he disliked us for being lackadaisical, disobeying regulations, and because we followed orders begrudgingly and often mockingly, especially since most of us hated the service, which he seemed to sense. Though everyone knew my situation, he was hardly sympathetic, and rarely gave me a weekend pass.

Arriving at the base on foot without a pass after hours was a serious offense. Wobbling in drunk was even worse. But, curiously, AP's at the gate always waved in motorists like me without checking our passes. They probably assumed that we were officers or non-commissioned officers who didn't need passes living off the base, I surmised. Or checking drivers inside the long line of arriving cars would take too long, I eventually concluded accurately.

Whatever the case, I always held my breath whenever I arrived Monday mornings, shortly before roll call. I also always wore my long coat and particularly my hat which contained a silver, musical lyre that resembled officer's bars. In fact, mistaking me for an officer, AP's often saluted, which I returned, then smothered my laughter with a pretended coughing attack.

Trudi's poor parents refused to accept free coffee and tobacco from me, even at a reduced price, which I considered admirable. Considerably loving, they deliberately paid the full price in German marks, in order to help us, which Trudi and I appreciated. Suffering from asthma after surviving four years fighting on the Russian front, her father worked as a plumber for a large firm and managed to sell most of my excess and odd goods to his fellow workers, which also helped.

The Renault was a godsend. It help me earn badly-needed money, saved me from walking back and forth to visit Trudi and erased the risk of getting caught climbing over the fence. But one day the inevitable occurred, which caused me more stress and grief. The car refused to start. A car-owning bandsmen towed me to Herr Vulmer, an old, reputable mechanic. Though desperate for business and reasonable, instead of junking my faulty generator and alternator for replacements, as we do in America, he offered to *repair* both at a reasonable price, which I accepted thankfully. But although I saved money, tying up the vehicle for two weeks erased a good chunk of my black market profits for that month.

When Trudi reached her ninth month, we rented a strafe-filled house in a town closer to the air base, and I was thrilled when my son was born without complications. But inexperienced and careless about birth control, we took chances. Reusing condoms because I couldn't afford to buy new ones, led to the inevitable. Trudi became pregnant about a year later, and although equally happy that our daughter was also born without problems, our financial situation worsened.

I avoided getting caught black marketeering, and never told my parents about our impending marriage or their grandchildren until we were officially married *according to regulations*. Although stunned, they surveyed the ordeal, eventually took us into their home after we arrived in America, but we weren't destined to get along.

My mother resented Trudi for taking away her son. Also, she assumed that Trudi deliberately allowed herself to become pregnant in order to escape the War's ravages and live a better life in America. Consequently, she treated her like a maid, which *I* resented and protested, but always behind my father's back, because I was still secretly afraid of him. But although we never shouted at each other (nor was I that type), my mother always reneged on her promise not to tell my father. She even exaggerated such exchanges, because, like so many others in similar situations, she had no conception about the importance of "keeping one's word," or accuracy, I remember thinking regretfully.

Forever misinterpreting my complaints as disrespect, my father would rage anew, which humiliated me before my wife and children, particularly because I wasn't able to stand up to him yet, which puzzled Trudi, who was a staunch, proud German, and we resolved to move. Using my severance pay, I put a down payment on a Levittown home, which the government was offering to G. I's for low monthly payments, and we eventually moved in.

CHAPTER 25

College Revisited

RESPONSIBLE AND CLEVERLY RESOURCEFUL, I quickly obtained two part-time jobs at age twenty-five, advertised in *Newsday* for piano students, and was reasonably successful.

Like many veterans, I appreciated the chance to attend college on the G. I. Bill, applied to Queens College in Flushing, New York, and they accepted me into night school on condition because of my average high school grades. Maintaining at least a 'B-' average for thirty credits, would enable me to attend daytime college free, I learned, and I was thankful about only having to pay nine dollars a credit, which was outrageously reasonable even then.

Having scored high in music and English on a high school aptitude test, I chose to major in English literature, which I considered was a broader field than music, especially because it including philosophy, which interested me. I also decided to teach in high school and hopefully in college later, unaware how expensive that would be.

College scholarships were available, I also discovered, but for those who excelled during high school, not for the creatively gifted like me, especially considering my problems. Not until many years later, did I realize that, generally speaking, the creatively different and particularly the maladjusted and the sufferers, often make the best teachers and writers for many reasons, providing they overcame their hardships and difficulties, true in my case, and as long as they're not bitter. In fact, scholarships should *also* be granted to them first, not the superficial, mean, and those who can whip out a knapsack full of degrees and boast straight A's, which I also learned has no value unless the person does more with his/her life than just accumulate tons of money and material things. *The problem is that such scholarship givers are usually too conservative to understand this, and/or they follow conservative guidelines.*

Philosophy 101 was one of my first classes, which I'll never forget. Still innocent, naïve, and idealistic, I was the epitome of seriousness and determination, which is always a professor's delight. I recall staring curiously and almost reverently at our professor who was slightly older than I. Smiling while standing before the class, he introduced himself and welcomed us. He then asked everyone to do likewise up and down the rows and include where they lived, their major, and why they were taking the course, which they did. Afterwards, he randomly called each of us by name, one by one, without making a mistake, which amazed everyone, particularly me.

Though he never discussed metaphysics throughout the term, nor did I ask about God, the universe, or man, he appreciated my many stimulating questions about the philosophies of Plato, Socrates, and others. He gave me A's on both required papers and an 'A' for the course, which was so encouraging, that I almost succumbed to tears. I was so elated that, had I not been on speaking terms with we my parents I would have shared the good news with them.

Weeks later, though I completed twenty-seven credits, including many required courses in my major, I barely managed to maintain the needed 'B-'. Nevertheless, day time college seemed within my grasp. I only needed at least another 'B-' or higher in any three credit elective that I selected.

But instead of taking an easy course as others might have done in my situation, I was fanatically concerned about improving myself in all areas. Since I did poorly in math during high school, having failed intermediate algebra twice, I chose it as a refresher in order to prepare me for the more difficult math courses that lay ahead.

The day of the final finally arrived. Pleased about having improved my math, I had an eighty percent class average and only needed at least a seventy-nine on the final to get the desired 'B-'.

Finishing toward the end of the period, I handed my test to our young, female professor who had been correcting them all along. I waited nervously as she corrected mine. She handed it back, and seventy-eight upset me. But surely she would grant me the extra point, considering why I took the course, I thought, especially since, as an idealist, I believed that learning, not grades, superseded everything, and the course *had* taught me much that I didn't know. Besides, I didn't believe in grades anyway. I approached her desk with the test after everyone left, presented my case, and was staggered when she refused. She was like so many unsympathetic others in the world, I remember thinking. I even stooped to describing myself as a married veteran pinching pennies while struggling through college with the birth of my third child. "I can't afford to take another course," I insisted. Having to pay another twenty-seven bucks, would literally take food off my table, I suppressed. "What if I did and didn't get a 'B-'?" I recall asking, then it hit me. Why should she care? I also kept to myself.

She uncorked the old routine that giving me an extra point wouldn't be fair to the others.

I'm twenty-five, older than these kids and an outsider. I don't even know them, flashed some thoughts. "I'm sure they wouldn't mind. I wouldn't if you changed somebody else's grade under similar circumstances." It's no big deal, woman, I suppressed, but *No* stood firm.

I thought professors were liberal, I recall thinking, while we exchanged brief, awkward stares. No way will I ever be so hard-nosed as a teacher, I vowed. You've gotta have heart, like the song, woman. It's a question of having love for others. And you ain't got it, I dramatized inwardly. Where's all the love for veterans? I also wondered. Chalk up another lesson about unloving folks, I announced inwardly and left.

CHAPTER **26**

Reconciliation

SHORTLY AFTER MY FATHER TELEPHONED the house, talked to Trudi for the first time in almost two years, he appeared at a nearby restaurant where I was soloing, adding to my many surprises. I took a break, greeted him self-consciously and awkwardly, and sat alongside him at a nearby table. Hardly the kind to admit mistakes, apologize, or give in, he almost ordered me to "let bygones be bygones," and start anew.

Nevertheless, having also learned about the value of forgiveness, especially because of our imperfections and weakness as humans, I conceded. We talked briefly because I had to resume playing, and he left.

But pray tell, I remember protesting inwardly while driving home after the job. After all the grief you gave me about my clowning around and "lousy grades" during elementary school and average high school grades, you couldn't find it in your heart to praise me for making it so far at college? And no compliments about my improved playing? I added, all of which I verbalized to Trudi after arriving home that evening.

"People don't change," she insisted.

But highly perceptive, I couldn't disagree more. Maturing as we grow older, most of us do constantly, or at least we're capable of doing so, I thought even then. Sometimes we become forgiving and loving if we weren't before, untrue about my father, I realized. I had long since changed from being unruly during elementary school. Having matured, I was less superstitious than before, I also knew.

Looking back, I appreciated that my father forsook his ego and make the first move, but the world was full of negative souls like both my parents. But their lives weren't over. Both still had time to overcome their faults and grow before passing on, I knew, and we finally visited them with our children.

"See, I told you college wouldn't be easy," negative Mom contributed at the dinner table after I foolishly told her about the professor. "What if you fail that course too? Even if you pass, you'll still have a good three and a half more years to go."

No kidding, Ma, I kept hidden.

Weeks later, I took the easiest course possible, passed with a "B," and looked forward to attending daytime college.

Since the regular staff was stricter, courses would probably be more difficult, I predicted before starting a month later. So would competition from younger students fresh out of high school when professors marked on a curve. Having not attending a regular class for seven years, didn't help, I knew. Worried about failing, I felt pressured, especially since Trudi was counting on my success.

"So you can become a teacher and we wouldn't have to starve," she often fantasized aloud to me, unaware how little teachers were paid then.

Appreciating her dedicated support, I was convinced that professors along the way would somehow answer my questions about life, Jesus, and God.

CHAPTER **27**

Dealing with More Stone Walls

ATTENDING DAYTIME COLLEGE, I SOON found out that I needed to take two semesters of physical education for a degree, which even applied to older, married veterans like me. What about those with three children? How many more do I need in order get exempt from taking phys ed? I wondered. Who's running this college? I even grumbled inwardly. Although I respected the college's great staff, I was also annoyed about having trouble fitting the course into my schedule.

It's not worth wasting my limited studying and teaching time just to drive to Flushing to take such a worthless course, plus money for gas, which had risen to an outrageous sixty cents per gallon, I also thought. Most of my students claimed that they had such busy schedules (or couldn't care less about the piano), or were so indifferent and spoiled, that they would rather quit than change the lesson time or date, I also knew since it had happened twice.

Other complaints surfaced. I could get hurt playing basketball and football, I pictured, and decided to see a counselor about dropping the course.

Checking my schedule, the dean, another young female, kept insisting that phys ed was required.

"I know. I know," I recollect answering. Why do people keep repeating themselves? "So? Un-require it," I also remember responding agitatedly.

"I beg your pardon?"

Another stone wall, I announced inwardly, gave up, and left. Attending that class days later, I ran for a pass, missed the football, and it hit my glasses, which broke in two. Just as I anticipated, I thought, or had I purposely missed the ball in order to prove my own point, I also entertained curiously, already aware that most accidents were often deliberate, rather than coincidental.

Poor vision forced me to drive with one hand while the other hand held the lens to one eye. Since I couldn't afford new glasses, after arriving home, I snipped the heads off several pins which I threaded, glued, and reconnected the two halves.

Always pressed for time, especially since I was carrying eighteen credits, I was constantly speeding, and finally got caught one day. The State trooper handed me a ticket, which I had to mail in with forty dollars or appear in court. Choosing a different approach, since my writing had improved considerably, I attached the ticket (minus the money) to a nice sobbing letter explaining that I was broke working my way through college with a wife and three children, but to no avail.

Pay the fine or appear in court if I chose to defend myself, came the court's response in the mail.

What the hell do they do with all this money? unfolded more grumbling about the cruel outside world. Nevertheless, deciding to contest it, I squeezed the appearance into my loaded schedule. Who the hell is he that I have to stand up for him? I also suppressed, and considered remaining seated, when I noticed a policemen regarding me curiously, and I rose with a smirk. Eventually facing a rather distinguished man who reminded me of my unyielding father, I could barely speak, much less defend myself, except repeat what I had said in the letter, which I knew would sound like begging again.

Unsympathetic, the judge simply asked me if I were speeding.

Refusing to lie, that is, contrive a story, I admitted my guilt, was thankful that the clerk would accept a postdated check, and left. Trudi was furious with me for wasting the money, and rightfully so.

Weeks later, tired from staying up late writing an essay for my first English course, I ended up oversleeping. Since I was already tardy the first time I appeared in that class, I chose to speed again and a different state trooper stopped me.

"Don't you ever check your rearview mirror?" he inquired after studying my license and registration.

Why, is it dirty? I almost considered responding with a laugh, but apologized and decided on the truth. "I was studying," I answered sheepishly.

Puzzled, he eyed the opened book resting on the passenger's side. "You're reading while you're driving?"

No, I'm driving while I'm reading. "Yes," I admitted.

He did a double take. "You've *got* to be kidding. Are you crazy? Do you know how dangerous that is?"

You have to do what you have to do, I left unsaid and unleashed another respectful smirk. I briefly revealed my situation, added that I was a veteran, and he let me go. At least a few kind-hearted souls are around, I thought and continued toward Flushing.

CHAPTER **28**

Finally Dealing with Attention Deficit Disorder

SENATOR MC McCARTHY WAS STILL in the news the first day I attended history, which I'll never forget. After jabbing the politician, the professor began discussing the course, which he had outlined on the board. Having never taken notes, not even during night school, I watched curiously as everyone began scratching away feverishly, save me. These are just a bunch of high school kids, I rationalized. I'll remember everything, I assumed innocently.

After the professor finished, I *watched* him begin lecturing. I say *watched* because after the period ended, I realized that I hadn't assimilated anything. I didn't hear him? I questioned internally. How's that possible? How can I get through college with poor hearing? How could I afford to buy a hearing aid? I demanded, unaware that I had been day-dreaming throughout the period. Glancing at my neighbor's notes, I gathered that the professor had been discussing Chivalry. Realizing that I had been fantasizing myself as a knight rescuing a beautiful maiden for forty minutes, I almost choked.

Thank God, I can always read the textbook, I rationalized. What textbook? I questioned after noticing what resembled a title that the professor had written on the board. "Is that our textbook?" I asked a male heading for the door. What else could it be, dummy? I scolded myself.

Driving home, it hit me for the first time. I've got trouble focusing and I have a short attention span! I announced. Except for philosophy that didn't bore me, whenever I listen to the news, I rarely recollect anything, I realized. Though I remembered my mind wandering during night school, the courses had been relatively easy, I recognized.

More self-analysis revealed that I rarely paid attention when others spoke to me. I frequently blocked out their words or barely caught tail ends of their sentences, as if I secretly feared absorbing a scolding, lecture, or insult, I suddenly understood. If I grasped anything, I often needed seconds to recall their words in order to be sure what they had said. Sometimes I wasn't positive even then, and I was too embarrassed to discuss this with anyone.

The solution seemed simple, I announced to myself. Start concentrating on whoever speaks to you, despite how difficult, boring, or simple, from slow-speaking two-year-olds, to professors, I ordered, which I began, and was surprised how little outside information I had been retaining, which I had blamed on a poor memory and hearing. Because I could hardly concentrate on professors' lectures or summarize what was most important, I had difficulty taking notes.

One day, I learned that the college was offering limited, inexpensive psychiatric treatment for veterans. What a chance to learn more about myself, I exclaimed happily to myself, overcame some guilt that such treatment was for soldiers suffering from combat, not those who had it easy like me, and signed up. My therapist was a man in his forties whom I was supposed to meet twice weekly.

Ignorant about such treatments, I pictured myself lying down on a couch beside him, as I had seen in the movies. Instead, he had me sit before him, which surprised me, more so when he rarely said anything, except to urge me to describe my early life, particularly my relationship with my parents, which I found difficult. Finally complying, I felt guilty, like I was informing on them behind their backs.

Towards the end of the six months, he finally started speaking, that is, psychoanalyzing me, I concluded. He described me as sensitive and kind, which stirred something deep inside, since nobody had ever complimented me about anything. Listening to him review the cellar punishment, appeared to fill my eyes with tears. Crying at your age? What's the matter with you? I scolded myself, unaware that that was another one of my mother's favorite lines directed at my sister and me.

"Your parents did the best they could, raising you," he conceded, causing me to nod, although reflexively, because I was smoldering with resentment about how badly they did, which contributed to my lack of self-esteem and confidence, he detailed at great length. "They just didn't know any better. Your father domineered you *and* your mother, who apparently was suffering from delusions of grandeur," he explained, astonishing me. "And they were preoccupied with money and material things, which superseded everything in their lives, because both of them came from poor parents. Don't forget that even though you're in debt, you really had the luxury of being the son of fairly well-to-do parents. They didn't."

Huh, I responded internally. As he continued similarly, I remembered that except for my cousin Nicky's parents, I was unfamiliar with good, loving parents and secretly sided with my father when he criticized them for babying him. In fact, my father deluded me into believing that scolding, reproaching, and never praising me, was the best way to raise me, especially because I was constantly acting up in class. I even considered them great parents, until he mentioned that although my father rarely spanked me as a child and occasionally only cuffed me in the back of the neck as a teen, which was humiliating enough, he had abused me mentally.

My therapist also explained that getting constantly beaten up, even from my supposed best friend had caused me great suffering. Miss O'Melia had been very unfair, he added, surprising me again, since nobody had ever agreed with me about anything, particularly when I criticized an adult. "The O'Melia incident was traumatic, the final episode that caused you to retreat from reality," he continued, and elaborated how, under such circumstances I had sunk so deeply into the subconscious, that I blocked out sounds, why I hadn't heard the motor of the car that passed me on that fateful day.

That's it, I exclaimed inwardly, which seemed to relieve some tension in my perpetually knotted stomach, which I had never noticed before. Years later, considering such upsetting years during my youth, I felt blessed that I never developed ulcers.

"Shame and embarrassment wasn't the only reason why you deliberately withheld telling your parents about your two illegitimate children. It was your way of getting even with them. Subconsciously, you wanted to punish them for how badly they had raised you," he added, stunning me further.

Next, he discussed my inferiority complex, lack of self-esteem, negativism, and even paranoia. He also urged me to have it out with my father and anyone else that belittled or took advantage of me. "You have to stand up for your rights, especially because you seem to be a good person," he added, which almost aroused more tears.

What rights? I questioned myself, unaware what that was. "Oh, I couldn't do that," I nevertheless responded.

"Why not? You've been complaining about him for weeks."

"Yeah, I know. Maybe I was hard on him because sometimes we had fun together. He always took me fishing. He let me raise chickens in the back yard. We used to play Ping Pong, pool, and,

and—" Realizing that I was trying to protect him, I broke off, especially when he simply regarded me during a long pause, and I looked away.

Aware that he was right, I flushed, then pulled myself together. "Complaining about him isn't my fault," I responded, unaware that I still had trouble eyeing anyone, directly, especially an adult. "*You* asked me to discuss him," I admonished, astonishing myself for having never openly scolded an adult. I was about to apologize for seeming ungrateful for his help, when he smiled during still another pause.

"Try," he urged gently, leaned over and touched my arm with sincere affection, which practically staggered me since except for my classical teacher and my Uncle Orlando who was a happy, loving man, no one had ever done so. "You need to do it for your own benefit. Your own soul," he inserted.

Whatever that is, I thought.

"And stand up against anybody else that belittles you," he urged so friendlily again that I burst into tears, shocking and embarrassing me, especially when he embraced me, and we parted soon afterwards.

Days later, I received a letter from his superior stating that I wouldn't need any more therapy, which disappointed me, mostly because I felt myself emerging from myself.

Weeks later, I visited my parents with my family. The opportunity to have it out with my father arose when both of us happened to be in the basement. I remember watching him head for the stairs under the dreary electric light, which hardly illuminated such dismal basements. "Dad."

About to ascend, he paused, eyed me, and I trembled.

Looking away, I pulled myself together and managed to regard him briefly. Go for it, I ordered myself, and quietly started complaining how badly my mother had been treating my wife "like a maid," I added, shakily, and he frowned. Talking to him in this manner and tone, which I had never ever done, sounded like someone else had taken over my body, I noted curiously.

"Oh, really?" seemed to sting my abdomen. "Is this what they're teaching you at college?"

Don't answer that, I commanded inwardly, which I had trouble obeying, much less continuing. "And, and you've been on my back. All my life. About my conduct in class, my carelessness, laziness. Since I was boy," I hurriedly gushed. "Belittling me, no, domineering me," I choked out almost painfully. "Never praising or complimenting me about anything."

Narrowing his eyes, he stared curiously. Wrinkles filled his forehead.

"Because you could never did anything right, still can't. That's your problem."

Bullshit, I suppressed, considering that I was succeeding at college, but another thought interceded. You're lucky I'm not violent or I'd carry you up the stairs and dump you outside, I also withheld, since I was quite strong having wrestled throughout high school and during my first year at Champlain College. But what would that prove? I asked myself as he continued glaring at me. "Really?" I recall managing to reciprocate almost in his tone, despite struggling to stop trembling.

"Really," he reciprocated, which seemed to have more body. "Thanks."

"You're welcome. This is the respect I get for feeding your family and letting you live in my house for months? For a measly hundred bucks a month?"

What's so measly about a hundred a month? flashed anther thought. You should've let me stay for nothing. Which I would have done for you had I been in your shoes, I didn't verbalize. Staring at a long crack in the cement floor, I was surprised. Despite frequent and lengthy philosophical discussions with fellow veterans on campus, I had more trouble than ever pronouncing words directed to him.

"All the sacrifices I've made for you, feeding and sheltering you all your life?"

Still unable to eye him squarely, I turned away. Momentarily stumped for words when he went into his "lack of respect" routine, I almost considered apologizing, when a belated answer came to me. "Isn't that what's expected from parents?" I interrupted him for the first time ever. I always treated you like you were a god, I remember thinking. Focus. Don't let him throw you, came more internal ordering as he continued rambling similarly. "Respect's got nothing to do with it," I finally threw back at him, which he ignored.

"Kids," he sneered and repeated a previous vow about not wishing to help me, the grandchildren, or my sister, financially. "You're all on your own now," he reemphasized, angrily. Shaking his head, he turned away, and ascended the stairs, which upset me further.

Kids? I questioned, despite feeling relieved that the ordeal was over. Is he kidding? I asked the banister. I'm married with three children and I'm responsible, I praised myself. I thought he was *finally* starting to respect me. He still considers me a kid, I reemphasized internally with disbelief and entered the kitchen.

Weeks later, was when I concluded that I had little to learn from him, especially because I sensed that he was still egotistical, intolerant, and prejudiced against everyone except Italians. But I still hadn't learned that those who dislike money like me, frequently waste it, blow it away, and are usually forever broke, which had already occurred and was destined to continue for practically the rest of my life.

Today, though I still consider that he had more to learn from me than vice versa, I realize that he represented the practical, steadfast, conservative qualities which probably helped temper my often rampant idealism. I also learned that although therapy is helpful, since we can't undo what really happened, past scars are never forgotten or erased, but are destined to haunt us forever, probably even in the next world.

CHAPTER **29**

Choosing to Learn, My Way
and Flunking out again

DESPITE MY MONTHLY G. I. allotment and earning from piano lessons and playing piano with various groups for weddings, private parties, and at different restaurants, I could barely meet mortgage payments. Often, our family simply ate potatoes or beans for days. But others have suffered and are suffering more than you, I reminded myself again.

As the weeks passed, my short attention span eventually lengthened. Concentrating better, I comprehended more whenever others spoke to me, and when I listened to the radio or read. Lacking time to practice on the old upright my father had given me, which was hardly worth his repeated praise about its value (as if he had given me the world, I always thought), my playing also continued improving, which elated me.

Continuing to advertise in a different newspaper, I acquired more students along the wealthier North Shore, but because most didn't practice, I felt guilty about charging five dollars an hour, good money then, that is, until I remembered how poor I was.

Though I couldn't play the accordion very well, because I knew the instrument's fundamentals, I got a job teaching it to beginners at a music studio all day Saturdays which helped me buy food. I spent most Sundays with the family at home, swimming at Jones Beach during summers, or strolling along the beach during the winter, if I could spare the exorbitant seventy-five cent toll. Otherwise, I took them for a drive, if I could afford gas money.

Taking the usual required courses during my first two years, once again I eked out about a "C" average to stave off probation. I'm the gentleman "C," I mused, and soon started taking courses in my major and minor, English and Education, respectively.

Naively assuming that most professors were as liberal and intellectual, like my philosophy teacher, I was elated that "The *Bible* as Literature," was offered that September, and signed up for it. Still impressed with such a brilliant faculty, I thought that I had finally found a professor who would answer some of my pressing metaphysical questions.

Having already established a reputation amongst some of the faculty for asking questions (and causing heavy head-turning from the younger, note-takers), I started unloading on the first day. "How do we know that the *Bible* is God's word? What proof is there?" I asked the elderly professor who was a distinguished rabbi with wavy, white hair.

"That's a controversial question," I remember him responding with a smile. "Many believers have faith that it is."

"Does the *Bible's* existence prove that God exists?" I asked, warmed by his pleasant smile.

Heads turned to eye the bespectacled, older, slim veteran with the wavy black hair and a slight bump halfway up his nose who always sat in the rear in order to eye the gapers back. Once I even placed my thumb on my nose and waved my fingers at a male who had been smirking me to death. Sorry to interrupt your fierce note-taking, pal. This ain't high school, I even dramatized to him, internally.

He faced forward, frowned at the professor, as if he were expecting him to agree with him, but the man either didn't notice him, did, and was kind enough to ignore him.

"I really can't answer that. We're not delving into theological philosophy," the professor eventually answered me.

Why not? flashed more disappointment.

"We're studying the *Bible* as literature," he reminded me, as if he had read my mind, and the young man turned back and threw me a sarcastic nod, which was my turn to ignore.

Shit, another dead end, I reflected. That ends that, I added, except for discussing similar questions with a few interested veterans between classes.

Several of them agreed with me that were God nonexistent, nothingness would prevail, save cataclysmic explosions at best, much less the universe and man, but despite exchanging such philosophical viewpoints with them, I felt unsatisfied. Furthermore, though I tended to be paranoid, I sensed that some of them considered me strange for discussing such matters, especially those who were pursuing business degrees.

Accepting that I *was*, one day I decided to approach my education and learning differently. Why bother memorizing who authored what, when, or why, much less periods like Romanticism, Victorianism, the Classical Period and related studies? I questioned, since such matters seemed meaningless and unnecessary. Learning for the sake of advancing intellectually and morally, was all that mattered, I concluded. Besides, didn't I have the right to choose how I wished to be educated? I asked myself rhetorically, unaware that I was reasoning idealistically, not logically or practically.

Though I marveled how Milton treated the paradise lost issue in his so-named epic, including his conception of Adam and Eve, Satan, and God, the work didn't answer any of my burning, metaphysical questions. I also enjoyed Shakespeare's sonnets and particularly his plays, which delved into the many different aspects of human behavior such as ambition, revenge, lust for power and what many religions consider sinful. I had even followed Shakespeare's great advise that being true to oneself prevents us from being false toward others.

Amazing how we often *really* know how to behave and act, intellectually, but can't because of our emotions and other reasons, I thought concerning *Hamlet*, unaware that I was describing myself. I also recognized irony, jealousy, and injustice in *Romeo and Juliet,* plus negative ambition in *Macbeth.*

Lost in my idealistic intention to learn and prevail *on my terms* rather the college's, I didn't discover until much later that in order to receive a BA degree, I also had to pass "The English Concentration," a final test, based on all the English electives that I had taken.

I continued maintaining a 'C' average into my senior year, attended summer school in 1958, and was proud that I had completed four years of college in three.

Pleased about having learned much about myself, life, and others, especially from reading other greats like Steinbeck, Maugham, and others, I knew I had matured considerably and felt confident about passing the test.

On test day, I sat in a room with undergraduates taking similar tests in their fields. Watching the proctor hand out the different tests, I suddenly experienced apprehension, as if I anticipated my own denouement. I received my test, scanned the questions, and was stunned. Titles, authors, and background information was naturally required, precisely what I had ignored. Having been seeking only insights about human behavior and philosophy, as if writers were speaking to me, I failed.

The test was unusually hard, I rationalized afterwards, and convinced myself that the next one given six months later, would be easier, hardly studied, and failed again. The hell with it, I announced inwardly. I'll try to get a teaching job, without the damn degree. It's not the stupid piece of paper that counts. It's how much you've learned—grown—I stormed inwardly, like a typical idealist.

Twenty nine years old in 1959, I was three months behind on my mortgage payments again. To prevent foreclosure, I had no other choice but to work two jobs while waiting to retake the test. The following year, during the hippie movement, the Vietnam War, the threat of atomic warfare, and the nation's racial problems, I was overjoyed upon obtaining a teaching job because of the teacher shortage.

And you got it on *your* terms, without the damn degree, I announced triumphantly but innocently, forgetting how much the real world believed in the value of a degree, nor that I had been awarded five classes of the most abusive eighth graders imaginable.

Entering my homeroom the first day, I had to fight my way through wholesale chaos. Boys were fighting, throwing girls' pocketbooks out the open windows, cursing, spitting, and whipping erasers and chalk back and forth at one another. Girls were screaming, and so on. One look at me raging at them to stop, and the rampaging continued. Though I finally established order after physically restraining several males, such misbehavior was destined to continue throughout that year, particularly if I arrived seconds late to my homeroom. Welcome to the real world in education, I recall finally declared inwardly.

Weak in grammar, which I had failed in my senior college year and never retook, I naïvely decided (that is, *idealistically*) to ask my English associates for help conjugating difficult verbs, determining correct usage, and so on, which proved to be another mistake. Discovering that some of the young English staff either contradicted one another or were just as stumped as I, including even the department chairman, I was dumbfounded. Don't they care? What the hell's going on? I wondered.

Two other eighth grade teachers had long since solved the problem. Ignoring the course's outline, they had stopped teaching grammar altogether, they told me. Learning as much as I should have done during college (but knew that I had budgeted my time wherever I thought best, and had no regrets). In fact, I soon realized that I knew more about grammar than the staff and even the chairman. Therefore, realistically, I should replace him, I mused with a laugh. Yeah, sure. That ain't the way the *real* world works man, I dramatized inwardly again.

Nevertheless, the District didn't rehire me after the school year ended, meaning, that they fired me, along with half the young staff, the epitome of my surprises, especially since I sensed that many were good teachers. Aside from knowing my grammar, I had even managed to control my unruly classes, had a good rapport with them, and rarely called in sick, which saved the District money. For this and other reasons, rather than getting fired, the District should have given me a raise, I protested inwardly.

After learning that firing newly-hired teachers was common, I suspected some underhandedness, and was right. To save money, the Lake Ronkonkoma District chose to replace new teachers with similar, inexperienced beginners. Students were the losers, I recognized, and my wavering idealism dropped a notch.

Though the firing rattled me, despite living in what was considered the suburbs then, we had planned to move in order to raise our children in the peaceful country anyway, I told myself, and we eventually sold the Levittown house at a small profit. But impulsive, after driving upstate with my family, I bought on first sight, a picturesque but old, run-downed farmhouse with fifty acres. Though sturdily built, it needed considerable work to modernize it, I barely noticed. Mr. Vanderpool, our shrewd but greedy, resourceful and shifty real estate agent, the only one in what was a microscopic town, claimed it was a steal at $5,600.

I put $600 down, which consumed a good chunk of our profit, and we moved in two weeks later. The rest of the money started dwindling fast as I began singlehandedly remodeling the large rooms, which included removing chimneys hanging precariously inside, replacing the downstairs toilet, and so on, unaware that Vanderpool forgot to tell us that the farmhouse needed a new roof.

Nevertheless, handy, clever, and relying on my unusual energy, I continued buying materials from the local hardware store and began constructing kitchen cabinets. Replacing the pot belly stove in the dining room with a new furnace in the basemen consumed another portion of our profit.

But I had other problems. None of the surrounding school districts would hire me without a degree, and I couldn't retake the English Concentration for another five months. Running out of money, I started searching for a part time job. But the nation was in a recession, and I soon found myself unemployed and ineligible for unemployment.

Meanwhile, I worked into the wee hours finishing the cabinets, installing some new windows, and changing light fixtures. I replaced galvanized pipes with copper and bought new doors for the front and back. Banging out old plaster from the walls with a hammer and sometimes even an ax, I spent weeks filling my lungs with dust. Sheet rock came next, which I bought from the local hardware store (where I was now blindly charging tools, paint, sinks, and even a new tub), then spackling, wallpapering, and so on.

I also borrowed money from the local bank in order to pay for a new septic system and bulldozing, which included filling the holes in our long driveway.

Once again falling three months behind in my mortgage payments, I panicked and borrowed money from Beneficial Finance Company at an exorbitant twenty percent interest.

The winter seemed to be approaching fast. Having removed all the hanging chimneys, I needed to add heat in the three upstairs bedrooms where my four children were sleeping or they would freeze.

A sympathetic neighbor, who had suffered the same financial strangulation when he was young, showed me how to install the baseboard system and helped me rewire the faulty wiring as I continued charging materials at the same hardware store where he worked.

Now a workaholic, I was obsessed with tackling and completing one task after another without taking a break or a day off. Nevertheless, I squeezed in time to study the different periods, dates, authors' names, and so on, namely all that I had ignored. I retook the Concentration proctored at Cornell University, passed, and received my B. A. Degree soon afterwards. Elated, I also obtained a job teaching secondary English at a high school that was relatively near. The only problem was that the job wouldn't start until September, 1961, six months away. My indebtedness would not only worsen by then, but I could never hope to eliminate it on a teacher's salary.

Earning money playing piano in the surrounding area on weekends, hardly helped us financially. Unable to find a part time job for months, I was so broke and in debt, that I remember lapsing into despair. I couldn't even afford to buy gas to *drive* my family to a movie or restaurant, much less pay for either. I was also declining invitations to attend faculty parties for the same reason. Dinner at a teacher acquaintance's house was also out because I couldn't afford to buy extra food in order to reciprocate.

My gas needle was constantly on 'E.' Fearful of running out of gas before arriving somewhere to play, I was constantly coasting down hills in neutral and holding my breath. Though I appreciated that a local gas station owner allowed me to buy gas on time, I resented him for being rich.

Booking a band at a restaurant wasn't so simple, especially if the manager left for the night without out paying me. Unable to pick up the check for until Monday, according to the bartender, I couldn't pay the musicians, which was embarrassing. Worse, sometimes I even had to borrow a few bucks from them in order to buy enough gas to make it home.

Vaguely aware that I had made the wrong choices, I was angry at indefinable others. I blamed capitalism, the greedy rich, and the government for my plight, particularly Vanderpool who talked me into buying the farmhouse and never told me about the leaky roof. I also resented him for becoming rich from capitalizing on selling cheap but equally rundown homes to young, innocent buyers like myself.

I considered going on welfare while waiting to start teaching, but Trudi adamantly refused, and I regret not being strong enough to override her. I also regret not renting first, and saving up enough money to buy a nicer home.

CHAPTER 30

Secondary Level Teaching
During the Early Sixties

SEPTEMBER ARRIVED. AT AGE THIRTY-ONE in 1961 I finally started teaching senior English at a high school in a city containing about fifty thousand inhabitants.

During that time, the youth were so disillusioned about the Vietnam War, racial problems, and the establishment, that many seniors at the high school, were forsaking college, and dropping into my "average and below" classes that were swelling to thirty-five students or more, which included the unruly, the rock and drug enthusiasts, and "the couldn't care less contingent."

The sexual revolution had replaced decades of taboos and secrecy, and promiscuity, drugs, and ear-shattering rock were rampant, which seemed to belie the peaceful farm lands and picturesque countryside. Kicked out of homes, many teens of both sexes were cohabitated in communes deep in the nearby woods, that is, in abandoned hunters' cabins, lodges, or shacks, until police or owners of such hovels, dislodged them, or forgiving parents took them back.

Older, tenured teachers avoided such coronary-inducing classes which department chairmen bestowed upon young, idealistic teachers like me. Given such bandits, I entered the classroom armed with my incorrigible idealism and dedication, and they usually responded with head-clunking their desktops in order to catch up on badly needed sleep.

Nevertheless, despite so much negativity, including my own problems of borrowing money so that I could continue killing myself remodeling the farmhouse, I forced myself to be positive and upbeat. Nor did I have favorites, which I disliked about my elementary school teachers. In fact, I had compassion for all of them, even the unruly, who reminded me of myself during my difficult elementary and early teen years, when most of us need considerable help, guidance, and love.

Though I didn't follow any traditional religion, I continued to believed in Christ's teachings, followed Christian values, and considered myself deeply spiritual and religious, as if I were a clergyman without being one. Deep inside, without understanding why, I sensed that, for what lay ahead, *I,* in particular, needed to continue striving to be moral beyond reproach, which seemed more logical than maintaining superficial values, or lapsing into lying, cheating, and stealing, et cetera. Anybody could do that, I thought, almost enjoying the challenge, as if I were defying evilness. No way can they corrupt me, I even reflected, as if I were addressing so-called demons. What the hell do you mean? I even recall asking myself.

I had long since concluded that physical life's challenge was to rise above functioning like an animal. In fact, the Creator seems to have placed animals here in order to show us that we *shouldn't* be animalistic and kill each other, like some of them do for food.

Wherever I played piano, whether in a bar or a restaurant, though I often attracted women during my renditions of slow love ballads (Men usually prefer something loud and fast), I refused to cheat on my wife, even when our marriage began to sour. Because I believed that people often marry for important spiritual reasons without realizing it, especially to help one another, I frowned on divorce unless serious physical or mental abuse was involved. (Years later, I was disappointed when the new generation began divorcing one another for little or no reason, which eventually contributed to the breakdown of the family unit and persisted for years.)

I tried to teach my unruly students how to improve their reading, writing, and speaking. (The latter was the most challenging.) They fought back with disinterest, disrespect and apathy. "Who cares?" they often unleashed.

"You should, because you're superior to animals, and should take advantage about what you're capable of accomplishing," I often answered.

"Oh, man, gimmy a break," I usually absorbed and similar retorts.

Often arriving "zoned out" in class or laughing uncontrollably from smoking pot instead of eating breakfast, several tried to sell me marijuana and whatever they could steal from anybody, from a hammer, to small electrical equipment like drills and sanders from BOCES, a nearby technical school affiliated with our school. My lectures about honesty or the disadvantages and consequences of dishonesty, usually inspired them to drop their heads to their desktops for coma-like departure.

"I'd beat the shit out of them, if I were in your shoes," macho males sometimes advised me after learning what was *really* going on in school in our district and in many others throughout America then.

Thanks for such loving, valuable advice, I always thought.

Though some teachers thrived on being policemen, I rarely put students on detention or turned in the marijuana maniacs or suspected thieves. Anybody can do that, I knew. The trick was trying to stimulate them to learn for learning's sake, to care about themselves and others, and to improve their values.

For class attention and mine, many of the unruly often lied or enjoyed "putting me on" about everything. In fact, most of them didn't know how often they lied or the concept of it. Not the informing type anyway, I wasn't anxious to waste time helping administrators catch and indict the males smoking pot in the lavatory, trying to sell me drugs, and so on, especially after such students trusted me enough to reveal so much about themselves, and I eventually became a father and psychiatrist to many of them.

One episode exemplifies how misguided many males were then. One day, I was sitting behind my desk filling out one of countless forms for the administration after school. In walked Tony who approached and offered to sell me a drill he claimed he had found, and I couldn't tell if he was telling the truth or lying. "You mean you're low on drug money?" I teased and he laughed.

"It's a nice drill. Cheap. Five bucks, like, you can use it to work on your house, man."

"Sorry, Tony. No way. We're not supposed to buy anything from students. You probably stole it, anyway."

"No, man, honestly. I found it."

"Don't you mean *dishonestly* you stole it?" I questioned, frequently using facetiousness as an escape during such boring incidents, and he laughed again.

Finishing the last entry, I finally looked up and eyed him and the drill. "Okay, I'll bite. Where did you find it?"

"In this car, man."

I regarded him curiously and he looked away briefly. "You're kidding. What do you mean, you found it in this car, son?"

"This car was parked a couple a blocks from here. The door was wide open, man. The drill was layin' on the passenger's side, so I took it. Not bad, hah?" he asked, practically shoving it into my face.

Is this kid serious? I wondered. "*Lying*," I corrected. "Use *lying* for whatever is at rest. I went over that, remember?"

"Same difference, man."

"Not really. *Laying* is wrong in this case, son. Tony, you didn't *find* it. You *stole* it," I emphasized.

"No, man. I found it," he insisted.

I spent twenty minutes explaining the difference between *finding* and *stealing*, but to no avail.

"So, you don't want to buy it?"

"That's what I said, man."

"Don't expect me ta hand in no homework, man," he retorted with a laugh.

"No problem, man. Just don't surprise me. I don't want to get a heart attack," I responded and he left.

Encouraging them to read stories was challenging. Though most girls read them, and appreciated my sincere vigor, passion, and sometimes theatrics discussing them the next day, my scholars invariably greeted me with folded arms and staring. Most were too lazy, indifferent, or couldn't read, I eventually discovered (after having them read aloud individually in class), and I always wondered how they passed English before.

How are these bandits going to make it in the outside after they graduate? I also wondered. Not too well, although maybe better in heaven where speaking is impossible, I mused with a laugh.

Since I conducted my classes democratically and always gave them a chance to speak their minds, they often bombarded me with, "These stories are stupid, man. They don't make sense."

"That's because you're too involved with drugs, sex, and partying to understand what good writers have to say about real life and human relations—what's *really* going on in the *real* world," I often responded typically, as the girls listened curiously.

"Who cares about such crap?" was another variation, which I also tolerated (or I would have had to kick out or fail most for such disrespect).

"Obviously *you* don't," was my turn to vary, which invariably sent them into uproarious laughter. "That wasn't even funny," I would usually insist, since they laughed whenever I scolded them. Because of my unlimited energy, as a mild punishment, I sometimes went into my routine about the different kinds of humor, almost laughing myself upon hearing the usual head thumping.

Since few read the stories, *I* mostly summarized them myself, sometimes resorting to acting out the parts, as if I were monologizing on stage, which most seemed to enjoy, save for the usual hard-core rebellious or indifferent.

"Nobody even read the dumb story, man," was a different objection.

"You don't know that for sure, son," came more of the usual from me. "But this story isn't dumb. You just lack the background to understand it," I often dished back in my usual self. Then, lapsing back to facetiousness, I frequently added, "That's why they hired me. To teach you things like this, man. You see, I think you forgot. This is school. I'm your teacher and you're supposed to be the student, remember? You're supposed to be trying to learn from me, man."

"Okay, okay. Cool down. Whatever, man."

God, I wish the old man could hear what's *really* disrespect, I frequently thought during such exchanges.

"How's this gonna help us when we get out?" was their more serious complaint.

"Who said you're getting out? You have to pass," was mine, and laughter invariably resounded, especially because they couldn't outdo me verbally.

"This is a writing experience. You'll be graded according to how you summarize each story in your notebooks," I always explained seriously, which they never obeyed until ten minutes before I walked to their desks in order to check their notebooks which they usually left home. (Sometimes they used them for bases when they played baseball in the school yard, sometimes even when it was raining.)

Since I couldn't stop them from copying the summaries from obliging girls, much less fail most for never doing their homework, one day I decided on a different tactic one day. "Okay, I'll give you a half an hour to get your summaries together. You can even copy from one another. Cheat," I added nonchalantly and pulled up the shade. "You might need extra light," I explained, and they stopped talking and stared, in order to determine, if I were teasing or not.

"What did you say, man?"

"What do you mean?"

"Are you serious?" questioned another.

"That's cheatin', man."

"You're gonna count our grades and put 'em in your book man?"

"Yes," I declared. "I'm even giving you birds class time to copy from one another," I varied. "That's the kind of guy I am," I added and almost broke up.

Since they were fanatic about grades with only one objective— to pass "and blow this dump," another of their choice remarks, they went wild. Most rowdies started laughing giddily while copying the girls' summaries, until something unusual happened.

Vaguely remembering my discussions about the different stories, they started disagreeing with some of the girls' summaries and one another, which first started as a tease or a chance to flirt with them, I recognized. Since the notebooks were making the rounds, even between some of my worst bandits, many began jokingly criticizing one another's poor penmanship, poor writing, and so on, until wholesale indignation and offense broke out. "This is a piece of shit," I even heard amid the noise and confusing as they snatched notebooks from one another.

"No cursing or you're out, remember?" I managed to insert. Maybe such criticizing will motivate some to have some pride in themselves, I considered curiously.

"A sixty? How come you marked so hard, man," growled a toughie, after I started reading off their grades the next day.

"Because you were cheating, son," I answered.

Laughter ricocheted anew, plus more indignation, but at me, this time.

"You told us we could, man."

"But you never listen to me, son. Besides, you didn't cheat well enough, man."

More laughter banged the old walls.

"Check mine again, man. I thought I cheated the best," insisted another.

"I'll bet. You've had a lot of experience," I commented, stimulating more of the same.

CHAPTER **31**

Secondary Level Teaching in the Real World

ONE SENIOR APPEARED BEFORE MY desk just before I started class, one day. The guidance department had just transferred him into my class, and he handed me the slip to sign as all paused to watch curiously and listen.

"I don't know how to read, man. I can't read nothin'," he announced, absorbing so many eyes that he yawned self-consciously.

Neither can anybody else, man. So don't worry about it, I suppressed. *Anything,*" I corrected, as was my habit.

"Hah? What? Oh, yeah. Whatever, man."

"Not *whatever, anything,*" I enunciated.

"What?"

Tempted to answer *nothing,* I didn't want to confuse him. "What do you mean you can't read? You should be able to read by now. Some of you are faster than others," I added seriously.

"No, man, he really can't read," piped up another male sporting hair down to his shoulders.

"He's got dyslexia," a girl explained, and I soon learned that teachers had been passing him through the grades. One had just dropped him, he revealed, which I knew teachers had been unloading to me, via counselors, since I started teaching.

Some of them probably thought I enjoyed teaching rowdies, I often reflected cynically, unaware that it was because I was lenient and for other reasons.

"Can ya take me, man?" he inquired as all continued staring, and he handed me the usual note I frequently received from one of our counselors, which I'll paraphrase as follows:

"I know you've got thirty-seven kids, two beyond the limit according to our contract. But Bobby's needs to graduate. He's a good kid and won't give you any trouble."

Since I believed in helping others, especially such kids, how could I refuse? I reasoned, signed him in and eventually had to read every test to him, privately, word for word, plus the final, which included writing out his composition (as he verbalized it to me).

Ironically, trying to telephone parents about their failing, unruly, misguided son (or sometimes a daughter) was futile. Most worked during the day and were rarely home. Nor could I afford to pay for telephoning them long distance at night from my farmhouse tucked in the woods.

The school sent disciplinary letters and failing notices to such home, which such bandits often discarded before their parents arrived home anyway, teachers knew. Because of limited, classroom space for the next year, administrators frequently pressured teachers into lowering their standards and passing mostly everyone, including some of the worst students, which many of us did reluctantly, including me.

The Spelling Award for the most creative cheater went to a teen I'll call John. "How come you always lower your head to about an inch above your paper before writing the word?" I once asked him from my desk, some twenty feet away.

"It's my eyes, man. I need glasses."

Suspicious, because he always scored a hundred, I checked his desktop carefully one day. Finding none of the words written there, I returned to my desk and began dictating twenty common but difficult words to spell which the students wrote on a notebook sheet they torn in half lengthwise. Watching John behave similarly after each word, I stopped and reexamined his desk, which was still immaculate, I realized. Puzzled, I lifted up his paper which I analyzed close to my eyes, discerned barely visible indentations of the words, and was stunned. Apparently before the test, he had been placing the one half sheet upon the other, and, pressing down hard enough with his ballpoint, copying down all the words. Slyly removing the sheet containing the indentation before each test, he only needed to lower his head in order to read them.

I scolded him for cheating and gave him a zero. Suddenly catching on, his male cohorts gave him a nice round of applause, and my idealism dropped another inch.

Maturer than their male counterparts, most of the girls merely shook their heads, which I appreciated. How will they ever find good marrying material out of such a bunch? I often wondered. Wising up, I started dictating randomly-chosen words from the list. But half the class started failing, and I stopped the nonsense trying to teach them how to spell.

CHAPTER 32

Educators, Administrators, and Dealing with my Scholars

THOUGH TEACHERS WERE SUPPOSED TO attend conferences during Teacher Conference Day, I never appreciated having to listen to so-called educators speak, especially since they rarely had anything meaningful to say about so many problems in education then.

Most annoying to me was that instead of hiring local educators to speak or retirees who survived guns in class, drugs, and whatnot, in New York City, the District was forever locating and flying in only *male* educators whom they paid well to do so. Many school districts throw their money away on such nonsense, why they're broke. Since such educators always possessed long lists of degrees, the public and some teachers were thoroughly impressed or fooled.

Apparently, such male educators appeared to impress many young, female teachers in the audience who I sensed were so happy about supplementing their husbands' income in those days, that they always applauded them wholeheartedly before and after their speeches.

Such educators invariably started with a stupid joke, then apologized *for never having ever taught in secondary school,* which always floored me. How the hell can they know what's *really* going on in the classroom, much less advise us how to handle the misfits, drug birds, and rowdies? I always protested (and my idealism finally disappeared.) Too bad the District doesn't hire me to lecture. I'd charge them half as much and give them the *whole* truth, I always mused.

Ironically, like many other teachers, I was so overloaded marking compositions, devising tests, and performing the usual clerical work associated with teaching, that I couldn't afford to waste my valuable time listening to them. Consequently, attending such conferences (usually held in the district's largest auditorium), as soon as I heard the opening joke, I would sneak out the front door with several other disgruntled male teachers and some female teachers.

Catching on, principals eventually began requiring teachers to sign in before and after such meetings. But checking for such disobedience became so time-consuming, that they gave up, especially after the Teachers' Union protested.

English teachers were also supposed to teach grammar according to our moth-eaten syllabi, which the District refused to pay teachers to revise, because they believed in raising administrative salaries rather than ours, as we all knew, especially because the public and even the media never understood that hiring more and better qualified teachers was the *only* way to solve many problems in education.

In fact, the Board and the newspapers in our District were pro-administrators and against teachers in those days.

Since few of my students did their homework or cared about anything (except partying, sex and drugs), I knew that trying to teach them grammar would also be futile.

Our District required principals or other administrators to drop in on us unexpectedly in order to critique our teaching, that is, check off on a sheet whether or not we used the board and/ or how we related to the students, and so on. (Although I always received positive evaluations, since administrators were supposed to find some flaws, once again in order to improve the quality of education, my evaluators sometimes criticized me for excessive lecturing on the left side rather than the right, or not writing on the board, et cetera, which I considered absurd.)

Afterwards, we met with the administrator who discussed our positive and negative points. We then signed the sheet which such administrators filed in our personal folders. Since such evaluations determined whether or not we received tenure and other considerations, new teachers like me considered them important.

Some of us like me even had special plans specifically used for such occasions, which tended to nullify the value of such evaluations. (In fact, everything was about appearances then, that is, mostly about administrators fooling the public and even one another in order to justify their outrageous salaries.)

Nevertheless, though aware that I was dedicated and a good teacher during those early years, I worried that one of my bandits would act up during such observations as a joke to impress his peers or the girls (that is, deliberately say something disrespectful or stupid, which some did in order to humiliate an undesirable teacher). Since I always established a good rapport with them, which was one of my fortes, I remember offering such classes a deal. I'd stop teaching them grammar, if they'd promise to behave impeccably and answer such questions as well as possible. After the happy, explosive cheering ended, they always agreed.

"How'd we do?" several rowdies usually asked me after such observations.

"Cool, very, very cool. Didn't realize how much you guys *really* knew about grammar."

Aware of my wit and facetiousness, they always laughed.

Though our District (and Board members) surely hoped to improve the quality of education, which was almost like a proverb at that time, their innovations were mostly short-sighted. One superintendent required principals to have us write the week's plans in a plan book, which annoyed many of us, especially me, particularly because it was redundant, considering my difficult students. Besides, our staff was mostly intelligent, dedicated, and conscientious professionals who knew what to teach, when, and to what extent, et cetera.

To spot-check plan books, this superintendent had principals load a batch into their cars and drop them off at his office at week's end. But he overlooked that close to a thousand teachers taught in our district. Deluged, he quickly stopped more of such nonsense.

But the award for foolishness occurred when the District hired a new superintendent who took his sabbatical before he even arrived and left with his family (at public expense) to "study Russian education," which upset many of us, considering his high salary, until we remembered that *female* secretaries ran the schools very well anyway.

CHAPTER 33

Teaching *Problems in American Culture* Instead of English

ONE DAY, I DECIDED TO teach and discuss what such students *really* needed to know, like the nature and consequences of lying, doing drugs, getting drunk, plus the danger of eating junk food, jumping in bed with one another, and so on.

I researched various subjects extensively, and, relying on my energy, lectured about how eating properly could minimize the chance of getting cancer, why they should stop smoking (and how to do so), and I even discussed the *Bible* and religion. I included arguments about politics, racial issues, the Vietnam War, life after death, and the importance of responsibility and upholding one's word.

I was soon pleasantly surprised. Most students, even some of the most notorious, stopped head-clunking their desks and seemed to appreciate attending class to listen to what became stormy lectures, particularly because I let them disagree and argue with me whenever they considered themselves right.

Looking back, I was the guiding, understanding parent they lacked but desperately needed during such controversial times. Some even brought in related newspaper articles, which was another pleasant surprise. The administration never learned that I changed courses, nor did any supposed reject ever turn me in for doing so.

"The dude is cool," I often overheard males comment about me.

They even invited to their parties in order to listen to rock, but I always respectfully declined (I'm too young to go deaf, I always thought with a laugh). Although I knew I was "easy" and that a good percentage took advantage of my good nature, others were dropping out of other classes in order to join mine.

Sensing that I was also giving them badly-needed therapy, sometimes I even allowed them to challenge me about my personal life, if I thought it would help them learn about life and the real world, or if it changed their negative attitudes and values.

Though I was really teaching them "Problems in America," a new course that could have been my forte, the administrator involved gave it to a young, beginning female who lacked the background, temperament, and imagination to capitalize on such a great opportunity. She was miserable struggling to teach such a controversial course, and students were the losers again. The basic problem was that instead of trying to place good teachers where they could utilize their talent for the students' benefit, most administrators were mostly involved with trying to further their themselves, and fooling one another, the Board, and the superintendent about the real problems in large rowdy classes like mine.

I didn't get better classes until years later, probably my reward for tolerating the so-called troublemakers, I assumed naively, because favoritism, politics, and other reasons had much to do with it. Nor did I ever put more than a few of the unruly on detention throughout my career. But why so-called educators bestowed teachers of elementary and middle school with aides rather than such classes like mine, never stopped amazing me. Surely, minds superior than mine obviously decided that younger students were more valuable than teens, I concluded cynically.

PART III

The Paranormal and Related
Spiritual Concepts

CHAPTER **34**

Connecting with some Unknowns?

SOMETHING UNUSUAL OCCURRED IN 1968, which many readers will consider paranormal. Stressed from having taught such classes during my first eight years, I had joined a Transcendental Meditation group two years earlier and was meditating twice daily, which helped me survive.

My children attended another high school which was on my way home, about fifteen miles from the farmhouse. Since they usually stayed late in order to participate in various activities, I remained at the high school where I taught and often corrected compositions or did other schoolwork before picking them up.

One day, my English chairman gave me permission to work in his small, quiet office on the second floor. Sitting behind his desk, I recall finishing several compositions, which contained my usual red marks, instructions, and suggestions, et cetera. Staring at the last paper I had finished, I paused to air my disappointment that four novels and a short story collection, which I had written and reedited had been rejected repeatedly for ten years. In fact,

I probably hold the record for discarding about a truckload of rejection slips during that time.

Maybe I should've been writing poetry all these years, I thought, and regretted not having done so during my twenties. Maybe I'll take a crack at it, I considered. Now? At age thirty-eight? Most poets publish manuscripts of poetry in their twenties, I reminded myself. Casually looking up, I was suddenly jolted.

What's that? I wondered, observing what resembled a row of translucent spheres.

Each about a half an inch thick, they were like raindrops or trinkets hanging down loosely from an invisible necklace. Squinting or rubbing my eyes didn't remove them, nor could I have been hallucinating from drugs which I never took.

They weren't cataracts that often veer left or right and float, which I wasn't destined to have until later in life. They're not in the physical world, I immediately realized. They're some kind of mental aberration? I asked myself. If so, what? I questioned, since I had never ever experienced anything similar. Surprised when they seemed to be looming from within, I tried unsuccessfully to blink them away again while I attempted to understand their significance.

Something or some force is urging me to write poetry? The Creator? Sure, I answered, sarcastically, aware that God didn't interfere in our lives. These spheres appeared from deep inside of me, and are agreeing with my intention? I considered next. Or they're some kind of negative force like demons warning me not to? I evaluated. Why would they care? What's going on? I continued to protest. Should I start writing poetry? I seemed to be asking myself and paused to consider doing so, which I knew could be a serious endeavor, because, depending on a poet's temperament, viewpoint, and other factors, it often involves lofty matters which could be philosophical and highly spiritual, the only kind I would attempt. Nor would I write verse or anything seemingly superficial except, perhaps, witty humor and satire, which were aspects of my personality.

Okay, why not? I finally agreed inwardly, nodded, and, to my astonishment, the entire line of drops disappeared, as if whatever had been responsible were satisfied, including my inner self with myself.

Or were the spheres some kind of reflection or energy that souls in the next world are capable of sending us? I evaluated for the first time ever. Which *they* turned off, after I agreed? Or had *I* turned them off? unfolded more uncertainty.

Returning to the same room, days later, I couldn't raise the spheres on my own. I corrected more compositions, and drove home, continuing to wonder if *I* had inspired myself or had been inspired, which I didn't share with anyone in order to avoid being considered weird or unbalanced. Besides, swamped with schoolwork, I ignored the matter, as if it were a harmless noise or other distraction. Smaller versions frequently occurred when I started writing poems, and, years later, when I began writing and re-editing this book, *including just now when I revised this very paragraph.*

Since we can sometimes communicate telepathically here, under the right conditions, why not between us here and there? especially since we're all souls, whether here in the body or there? I also considered for the first time. What else could the spheres have represented? Surely I wasn't superficial or foolish enough to play games with myself, I knew.

Today, I theorize that although we might not be able to communicate with souls in the next world, that is, talk back and forth, much less experience such spheres, I conclude that we *can* and *do* receive their energy, but to what extent depends on how advanced we are, morally, spiritually, and particularly lovingly here, *and precisely what we are doing with our lives.* In other words, we're fine if we truly believe that we are functioning as best and honestly as possible, doing something truly meaningful, if not for ourselves, others, especially for one's family. In other words, we're fine if we are truly decent human beings, doing the right thing, behaving morally, et cetera, as corny as all this sounds, especially since not everyone is in a position or capable of helping others. Some don't even wish to have a family, and so on.

If not, we should try and change our lives, which is not always possible. In fact, although I consider America a great country (despite our faults), assuming that we are truly free to pursue anything and accomplish our goals, if we have the ability and work hard at it, et cetera, *is an American myth, wishful thinking, even propaganda.* Obstacles include one's own incapability and/or handicaps, capitalism, interfering others, laws, inability to be in the right place at the right time, et cetera. In fact, this list is astronomical compared to the others that I cited.

The point is that instead of appreciating life which God gave us, some waste it doing nothing but loafing. Some are mean and selfish, and many of us are only concerned about money and acquiring material wealth, and so on. Others risk life in many ways including climbing precarious mountains, jumping off bridges at the end of ropes, and so on.

Ironically, some folks are naturally kind and loving. They're always willing to help others (true about some of the youth because of their closeness to the spiritual world, as I contend, and other reasons). Others have to work at it, especially if they have been suffering for any of many possible reasons.

To repeat, the better souls there are more apt to direct their energy towards worthwhile souls here, not the liars, cheaters, and the angry here. If those souls receive any energy, it would be from similar negative souls that have little energy which is true here. The good or decent are more apt to help those similar in kind, those with whom they are most compatible, not those possessing the negative qualities just cited. Nor am I implying that better souls shouldn't try to help weaker souls, the degenerate, and even the immoral when possible, but not at the risk of jeopardizing their own morals and/or integrity, et cetera.

Today, I also interpret the spheres as a way that good souls were inspiring me, but not necessary to write poetry, which few people read, but, rather to write what I consider is this philanthropic book. If valid, my theories will help many have a better understanding of how and why we should strive to become as positive and moral as possible in both dimensions, in order to overcome negative forces, and for many other good reasons.

Other kinds of communication seem possible between souls, whether between us here, or between us here *and* there. On two separate occasions while soloing on the ship, I took a nap (because I had to play late that night), and *did* hear loud words spoken which woke me from a deep sleep, words which alluded to something too personal to reveal now. They were so clear and resonant that I thought my roommate, a trumpet player sleeping in the upper bunk, had spoken, but he was snoring away. Nor did I ever share that experience with him either, for the same reason I mentioned before.

The incident is particularly significant because if souls are attempting to communicate with us from the spiritual world, there seems to be no set rule about how they might try doing so. It could be with images like the spheres, or simply having us *know* something which often occurs during dreams, or they could somehow manage to verbalize words, as I just described.

The point is, considering that throughout our history, including up until today, we have been trying to communicate with the dead (that is, *souls*, since we can't really communicate with the dead,) in various different ways depending on our culture's religious philosophy, why wouldn't we be trying to do so from there to here?

I also conclude that the deeper we reflect through meditation, the better is our chance to connect with them. In fact, we could be *evolving* to the point of doing so spontaneously.

On another occasion on the ship, after visiting St. Thomas during the day, I opened my cabin door. Because we lacked a porthole, I normally turned on the light, which I knew wouldn't bother my roommate who always napped behind a drawn curtain. About to do so, I was taken back immediately. The room seemed to be glowing. Stepping inside, I suddenly realized that all four walls were glowing with a continuously-connected scene of a typical island, which was more beautiful and magnificent, than the actual physical scene.

What in God's name—? I remember wondering. The scene even included the light switch on one wall and a calendar on the next. I'm hallucinating? I questioned, studying the rich blue water, the palm trees, and the sand illuminated from a vivid sun.

Touching the walls didn't disturb the scene, which I continued panning. My roommate was snoring behind his curtain again, and I rejected waking him for the same reason as before. Besides, it's internal, spiritual, I concluded. Only *I* can comprehend or see it, mentally, I sensed though I wasn't sure. Turning on the light will probably dispel it, I theorized, which happened when I did.

Did *I* create it, imaginatively? I queried inwardly. Or were souls from the spiritual world responsible? If so, what were they telling me, if anything? Maybe nothing. Or they were just saying hello? I even speculated.

Critics will probably argue that I imagined all these incidents or that I was hallucinating, which is possible. But I wouldn't have included such incidents in this book, if I thought so.

I have also experienced flashing images of strangers during the day. On one occasion after returning home, I was re-editing this book, looked up, and glimpsed a colorful image of a young woman standing behind a child who was sitting before her in my living room. Both were strangers. The woman smiled, and I remember both disappearing immediately.

Surely I could have created them imaginatively, but once again, why would I? Who were they, and why did they appear? Nor could I produce them on my own. Possibly they're souls sending me energy in order to help me write this book? I entertained again, particularly since I couldn't disprove this and because that would be something loving to do considering this book's importance. Besides, what harm was there believing this, as long as I didn't become superstitious, I reminded myself. The point is, debunking the unusual, the paranormal, or whatever we don't understand or whatever is contradictory or controversial, including the existence of a Creator, is the easy way out, I concluded and dropped the matter.

CHAPTER 35

The Blue Light and the Third Eye

SMALLER VERSIONS OF THE SPHERES continued to appear, intermittently throughout my teaching years (but not after I finished writing this book, which I consider logical and significant. Nor had I ever experienced the spheres while completing six books before this one.) They resembled dots or tiny sparks that glowed and quickly disappeared when I stopped thinking about them, namely when I wrote poetry or discussed the profound in class or with anyone, *not* when I corrected papers or when I was preoccupied with the mundane.

Meditating throughout my forties, had enabled me to survive teaching unruly students, and apparently the conditions were right for something even more unusual to occur.

Looking back, one night at age forty-eight, I left the house in unusually high spirits, and played piano at a nearby nursing home. After the job, I drove home feeling almost giddy from what appeared to be a natural high, nor was I aware that my pulse was in the comfortably low sixties, which I was to discover later. I retired with my wife in our upstairs bedroom and fell asleep.

Suddenly, what appeared to be a third eye opened in my brain, awakening me. I hardly had time to evaluate it when, with my regular eyes wide open, I watched panoramic sections of what I realized was the milky way, flash before me, simultaneously with each heartbeat, seven times before stopping. The stars disappeared and my normal vision returned. Once again, I was astounded. We have a middle eye? I evaluated, despite having heard that it was associated with the pineal gland. Was this an out of the body experience? I also evaluated.

I woke my wife, told her about it, but conservative and skeptical, she attributed it to a dream. Disagreeing, I decided to look up what others had to say about the experience. The following information comes from Ellie Crystal's Metaphysical and Science Webs:

> Humanity recognizes a third eye, which is connected or associated with the pineal gland, about the size of a pea, located deep in the brain behind and above the pituitary gland which lies behind the root of the nose. Some believe that it is a dormant organ that can be awakened to enable telepathic communication. Many consider it the spiritual eye, our inner vision, which has mystical powers.

Further on she maintains:

> The third eye development, imagination, and visualization are important ingredients in many methods to separate from the physical form. Intuition is also achieved through third eye development. Knowledge and memory of the astral plane are registered in full waking consciousness until the

intuition becomes strong enough. Flashes of intuition come with increasing consistency as the third eye is activated to a greater degree, through practice.

The third eye, the organ of spiritual vision, is intimately related to karma, as we become more spiritual in the natural course of evolution. When the pineal gland is lifted from dormancy, consciousness is raised from an emotional nature into an illumined awareness. If the pineal gland is not fully developed, it will be in the course of evolution. When our sense of ego and personality are set aside and we keep our mental energy intact, we can become conscious of the non-physical, our inner self, the subconscious, through different practices to activate the 'light in the head.

I appreciated her explanation, but was disappointed that the so-called third eye never opened again,

Another seemingly paranormal experience occurred, years later after we sold the farmhouse and moved closer to where I had been teaching. Still deeply in debt and struggling to make mortgage payments on our small house, I needed a shed for storing outside equipment, and decided to build it myself in order to save money.

Fortunately, the District began replacing the school gym's old oak wood flooring, and officials gave me permission to take all I wanted of long one by fours, which workers were discarding outside. Lacking a truck, I loaded the pieces on top of my car daily, which I transported home until I had enough.

Still a workaholic, which I hadn't learned to control yet, I couldn't afford to buy a circular saw, and spent all summer sawing the lengths by hand. Since I often frequented the dump for firewood, discarded wood, and sometimes piping, et cetera, I even picked up some used two by fours and windows which I repaired and installed.

By late August, I was about a half a dozen shingles shy of completing what was an interesting 12 x 18 foot shed, which was three stories high and contained four inch tongue and groove siding and flooring. Hoping to install the shingles on what I barely noticed was an unusually windy day, I lugged over my paint-speckled, wooden ladder (which I found at the dump and repaired), placed it against the shed, and brought over my tools, nails, and the shingles.

I started climbing up, when suddenly, a small blue light, about the size of a pea, glowed with unusual fluorescent intensity somewhere inside my left eye, which surprised me.

Now what? I wondered still again after it faded away, and I paused to evaluate it. I'm being warned? The wind is going to blow me off the ladder or off the roof while I'm hammering? I questioned internally, and another gust powdered my sunburned face and the siding with dust particles and dirt. Or I'm warning myself? I also evaluated while watching another surge of wind bent some distant trees.

Ah, what the hell, I'll just chance it, I first thought, anxious to complete the job. But what if that was *really* some kind of warning? I reconsidered because of past experience with the spheres. If so, who or what was responsible? Surely not God, I knew. Souls from the spiritual world? I ventured, again. Once again worried about becoming superstitious, I waited for the light's reappearance, so I could analyze it further, but it never returned. So, climb up and see what happens, I tempted again, but didn't want to seem arrogant and/or ungrateful if the blue light was truly a warning. What's the panic? my other self interceded, and reentered the house.

Several days later on a calm day, I stepped outside, gathered the same tools and shingles, and approached the ladder. Warily and hesitantly, I climbed up several rungs, paused, but nothing happened. I continued to the top, finished the job without experiencing the blue light, and descended.

Weeks later at a Transcendental Meditation meeting, I met a woman who experienced the same blue light during a similar, possible dangerous situation. Unfortunately, her situation escapes me, but knowing precisely what it was, is immaterial. She too interpreted the blue light as a warning, changed plans, and nothing negative occurred. Determining what would have happened had she chosen to follow her plans, is impossible, true about myself.

The point is, because she experienced what seemed to be a similar blue light, suggests that all of us might have the same ability, although meditating could have been a determining factor in both cases. Curiously, just now, as I was re-editing this paragraph, the blue light flashed and disappeared, meaning that I'm theorizing correctly? Or is this just my inner self playing games with myself, again? I couldn't help thinking again.

What about those who followed strong premonitions to change planes that eventually crashed? I asked myself. Weren't such premonitions similar to the blue light experience? I reflected. What about premonitions that *don't* materialize, like planes that *don't* crash, for example? I disagreed inwardly, struggling to understand whether *we* or souls from the next world warn us about possible dangers.

What about those who escaped death during hurricanes, earthquakes, 9/11, and so on? Were they warned? I still analyze today, and conclude that in the broad scheme of things—which we or God might be controlling—we pass on when it is our time, to paraphrase an old cliché. Apparently, in all such cases, it wasn't their time to pass on, for whatever reason, including that they still had more to learn here.

Though we're all part of God's overall plan, I speculate that *we* are subconsciously controlling when we should die, not the Supreme Intelligence, which has created us incapable of knowing when, where, or how. Surely we would behave differently towards ourselves and others if we knew, nor should we tempt fate, thinking we *do* know. Nor is this to say that we cannot sense or predict the end when our time draws near, which many of us have done.

CHAPTER **36**

Liars and Keeping one's Word

To REPEAT, THE UNIVERSE FUNCTIONS predictably and beautifully. Laws work consistently well. The exceptions await unraveling, explanation, or understanding. Our Creator doesn't interfere with our free choice. (Nor did It create us morally perfect which would have turned us into robots, eliminated free choice, and prevented us from developing on our own.)

Deception is non-existent. In other words, the universe doesn't lie. Most of us do. Average folks lie. So do car salesmen, mortgage brokers and bank officials, et cetera.

Presidents lie, unless insurmountable political factions block them from fulfilling their promises. We lie more than we realize, not just because being telling truth is difficult or because we're imperfect, but mostly for personal gain like money, to "save face," and countless other reasons. Consequently, most of us are out of harmony with the universe and the Creator.

Many of us lie continuously without realizing or caring about it. Catching ourselves on occasion, we consider lying "part of life" or trivial compared to what is *really* important—making money, as much as possible, which dominates many lives. In fact, some of us even commit murder for money or suicide if we lose great sums.

We all know that companies and others that advertise something is "free" is usually a lie. Since revealing the *real* truth would reduce sales, cause layoffs, and even bankruptcy, many companies exaggerate about their product's value or withhold information detrimental to sales, which is a form of lying. Were it not for consumer reports about products, certain companies would lie even more. I respect and patronize those companies whose products are so superior to others that lying is unnecessary.

Using trial and error, I finally figured out which company makes the most durable, long-lasting batteries for flashlights and gadgets. The point is, surely the CO and employees *also* know. Instead of improving their product, *the morally right thing to do* and carry to the next world, such companies continue wasting money advertising the lie.

Though employees should refuse to work for such companies, I realize that physical life isn't paradise. In fact, this is another *Catch-22.* Since such companies often can't afford to improve their product and would go bankrupt if they did, they continue lying which employees tolerate because they rarely consider such matters, couldn't get another job if they quit, and need that one in order to live.

The few new cars I bought, *never* lived up to getting their advertised miles per gallon. Assuming that car manufactures test cars on level roads, such advertisements don't include a car's speed. In fact, testing could be at five or ten miles per hour *below* the speed limit when, in fact, many of us drive *over* the limit. An honest advertisement should state how many mpg a car gets on a level road at precisely the speed limit on the highway or in town, or chose a different method for conveying the real truth instead of withholding pertinent information, which is a form of lying or what I call a sly lie. (It even rhymes.)

Another example of the sly lie involves television sets, which manufacturers measure diagonally and even include the border when advertising their widths.)

Sometimes we lie just to trap someone into telling the truth. Others lie to cover mistakes, to avoid getting scolded, or going to prison.

Many liars often forget which one they told to whom, when, why, and under what conditions, which they struggle but fail to hide, which some of us tolerate because we lie also.

Lying to protect oneself or another who has committed a crime is rarely justified, although sometimes necessary during harmless situations, (which we call "white lies"), that is, when telling the truth could hurt another's feelings about how they look or what clothes they're wearing, et cetera.

"Who cares about telling the truth?" my rebellious wonders invariably protested when I discussed the importance of honesty.

"You should," I often responded, which initiated another of my passionate lectures.

Shortly after my discharge from the service, I worked part-time as a door-to-door canvasser for a new vacuum cleaner company. Greeting the different homeowners pleasantly, which was easy for me (because I didn't have to be a phony), I would try and persuade them to allow one of our salesmen to demonstrate the machine. When they refused, the gimmick, as my manager had instructed me, was to offer them (usually women) a ticket to win a free one that we intended raffle off later, if they let us in to demonstrate, which usually worked.

"Who won the vacuum cleaner?" I asked him at a meeting after the raffle date came and left.

All laughed, including him.

"Nobody," he explained while fronting the group. "Are you kidding? We can't afford to do that," he told my astonished face. "Don't sweat it. You get an override for everyone you get in, remember?"

The lie's on me, I realized, flushing with surprise and innocence.

He urged me to continue the false promise. I agreed to his face, which was *also* a lie, or, perhaps, an example of a "rare, unusual, situation," because I eventually decided to reveal the blunt truth.

The only problem was that knocking on doors and announcing that the salesmen in my crew wanted to sell them a vacuum cleaner, received mostly "No thanks" and some slammed doors, and although I needed the job, I quit soon afterwards.

On another occasion, annoyed about so much lying, including my own, I needed to sell my car, and decided to reveal the truth about its problems. Advertising in the newspaper, I accurately priced the vehicle lower than bluebook value, adding that it needed a motor job, brakes, new tires, an alternator and a battery.

Ironically, most lookers were so convinced that I was withholding even more problems, that is, lying, that none were interested. Disappointed because I desperately needed the money (a familiar reason why we often lie), that I fell into the trap of withholding information, that is, lying. I re-advertised that the car only needed a motor job, and sold it soon afterwards.

The lessons learned was that in a capitalistic society, honesty can frequently cost us money, and blessed are those who would rather tell the truth and lose money, than lie in order to make a killing.

The point is, lying stunts intellectual growth and is one of the worst faults to carry into the next world.

Keeping one's word is another problem. Many of us forget or don't appreciate that unlike the animals, we have the ability to speak. Though we can explain where we will be at any given moment here, with whom, and so on, we often fail to uphold our word for any of many poor reasons.

Though I've changed the names, the following accounts, taken from my life, exemplify the consequences of failing to uphold one's word. Once again, they involve the curiosity of objects or things that offer us the chance to chose what is right or wrong, which cannot do in the next world.

Mike reneges on his promise to bring his wrench (the object) "right over" to Bob whose bathroom is flooding because he's trying (and failing) to tighten a loose nut with a pair of pliers. Mike can now choose from an almost endless list how to answer, including telling the truth or lying. So does Bob who might exaggerate (lie) in order to make Mike feel bad. Bob might even laugh it off, curse Mike, rage, including the promise to "beat the shit out of him" the next time they meet and so on. The point is, how each responds, why, and to what extent, depends on their characters, personalities, that is, their souls, at this point in their development, including how much love and compassion they have for others again.

The same is true about hypothetical Mary and Jane. Mary *promises* Jane to *invite* her to her *house* (which are physical and earthly matters mostly confined to our dimension rather than the next), then doesn't for countless possibly, poor reasons again, or lies, such as: she forgot, "got tied up doing something else," or didn't think Jane would mind. Nor does she telephone to explain why or to apologize, and so on. The truth is that she dislikes her, which I realize might be difficult to explain without hurting another's feelings in such a situation.

Though Mike and Mary might laugh off such incidents as being trivial, hurting or offending someone is an undesirable blemish to carry into the next world.

Blessed with answering machines, we record a promise to return calls, then don't, again for any number of poor reasons, which is another form of lying. Also blessed with the ability to speak, Americans and other English speaking nations, are *kinda* living in the *sorta* and *kinda* era. We *sorta* think, feel, worry, or *kinda* describe things that way. I *kinda* turned on the television last night, and *sorta* heard an announcer (supposedly representing our best speakers, or how could they have gotten such positions? I *sorta* always wondered). He was *kinda* describing the news and particularly sports events that way. The weatherman used *sorta* raining to describe *drizzling*, then a *high*, which he claimed was *kinda* moving in our direction, *if you will* or *sorta* understand what I mean. But how can a high *kinda* move towards us? I *kinda* remember thinking. It's either moving this way or not, *if you will* or *sorta* understand what I mean. It was *kinda* sad.

Like is another new phenomenon. *Like* I was *sorta* discussing this carelessness with a *kinda* friend of mine who isn't really friend, but *kinda like* somebody I *kinda* know, if you *sorta* know what I mean. I could *kinda* go into more detail, *like sorta* give you some more examples, but I don't want to *sorta* bore you, *kinda like*. Why not *kinda* reread these paragraphs to *sorta* determine how you *kinda* fit in, *sorta*, *if you will?*

If we're careless about telling the truth, punctuality, keeping our word, and speaking correctly, all relatively simple to maintain here, we will probably have difficulty communicating telepathically and adjusting to new and much more difficult laws there.

Believing that we inherit Adam and Eve's sin for disobeying God and eating the forbidden fruit sin (which would suggest an immoral God again), tends to excuse us for being sloppy about telling the truth, keeping promises, and much more.

CHAPTER **37**

The *Bible, The Commandments,* and the End Times

YEARS AFTER RETIRING FROM TEACHING, I moved to Miami and attended a seminar of orthodox Jewish scholars who were lecturing about the Dead Sea Scrolls during an open meeting. Afterwards, they mingled, informally, with the audience and began answering their questions. Approaching the crowd surrounding them, I couldn't decide which of many questions to ask them. Did they believe that Gabriel, God's supposed emissary, *really* spoke to Moses near the burning bush? I asked and all agreed, which surprised me.

Accepting the possibility that as a soul, Gabriel somehow managed to penetrate the physical world, I wanted to question why that couldn't happen today, but, unfortunately, they resumed answering so many other's questions, that we left.

The *Old Testament* contains many inspiring, moralistic stories and proverbs. But considering that it also depicts an angry Creator capable of punishing us for transgressions despite having created us with imperfections, suggests that the prophets colored it. That a supreme, loving intelligence would tempt Abraham to sacrifice his own son, is obviously a throw-back to the past when sacrifices were common. Were this story accurate, the great Creator of our universe and heaven would be unloving and unjust, and contradicted the Fifth Commandment.

Had I been in Abraham, I would have disobeyed, nor could I love an immoral God.

Though the Creator supposedly inspired the prophets and others to write *The Ten Commandments,* they seem to lack basic insights which one would expect from a morally perfect Super Intelligence.

To begin with, if the *Bible* is God's word, a loving God would have most likely inspired them to write in the positive, advising us what we *should* do, not what we *shouldn't* do, which is negative.

"Thou shalt not take God's name in vain," states The Third Commandment, which is poor writing or translating for implying that we could, if we had a good reason. As imperfect humans, are we *really* sinning for accidentally saying, "Oh for Christ sake," while experiencing intolerable pain? or for calling a love one's murderer a "Goddamn bastard?" Besides, how could such an advanced Creator be so insecure and sensitive that names would *really* hurt It?

The Fourth Commandment states that we should keep the Sabbath holy and not work, meaning that doctors shouldn't attend to patients desperately needing their care then? Or that we shouldn't try to save folks drowning during a sudden flood or those trapped in a burning building on the Sabbath?

The Sixth Commandment urges us to honor our parents. What if they were thieves, murderers, or they abused us?

How come God or the prophets overlooked, Thou should not lie, rape, be hypocritical, greedy, jealous, prejudiced, stingy, unkind, materialistic, or succumb to gluttony, et cetera? In other words, once again, if the *Bible* is God's word; if its authors are (were) reflecting God's laws, they should be flawless and impeccable.

(Instead of pounding the flock to accept the *Bible* as God's word, particularly the *Commandments*; instead of urging them to love God with all their heart, religious leaders would attract more followers if they were *honest* and courageous enough to discuss such flaws.)

Why most Jews reject Jesus as the Messiah is strange. According to the *Bible*, he spoke and preached like a Messiah and encouraged us to love one another, quite advanced then. He supposedly healed the lepers, raised Lazarus and himself from the dead, walked on water, turned water into wine, and so on. Even if all this cannot be proven; even if Christ never considered himself the Messiah, the point is, what looks like a tree, grows, seeds and flutters like one, must be one.

God could surely send mankind a different Messiah in the future, which would seem illogical since Jesus was supposedly God's favorite son who suffered here and might be still suffering there because we're still killing one another off and glorifying war. (Old war films turned into color for greater appreciation, which includes music, suggests that we're not anywhere near really loving one another, as previously mentioned.) Considering the attention, love, and hope that humanity has given Jesus for centuries, replacing him would be stupid.

Some believers in the "Second Coming" contend that Jesus will appear in order to save us from ourselves, which would seem unnecessary considering that his teaching and life convey how we should behave.

According to *Revelations*, Nostradamus, the Mayans, and others, Armageddon is near, including our government's collapse, all of this supposedly for our sins, failure to follow the *Ten Commandments*, Jesus' teachings, and so on. But having suffered the agony of creating the universe and us, wouldn't it be logical for the Creator to spare us?

According to the *Rapture*, God will resurrect Christ believers from their cemetery graves, which is impossible since most souls would have long since left for heaven, unless this refers to those trapped here as ghosts. Besides, the *Rapture* suggests the same unjust idea that whoever refused to accept Christ and/or his teachings would be damned. What if such folks were thoroughly brainwashed into believing another religion, feared death for not following someone like Hitler or Hussein, or lacked the intelligence to know any better, and so on? The possibilities are endless.

Worse, were the Creator responsible for Armageddon, those left behind would suffer from losing their love ones. Whisking away so many good souls would cause civilization's collapse, all of which would suggest that God is more immoral than the combined evilness of all our worst dictators.

For the reasons just cited, I disagree with the doomsday predictions concerning December 21, 2012. As we know, the media rarely reports good news, and I regret that they and others profit from alarming viewers about such negative possibilities.

Ironically, scholars have found no such negative predictions in Mayan literature, but, rather that a new era of positive, spiritual changes will soon begin. Besides, although planets, the sun, and other heavenly bodies are supposed to line up on the above date approximately every 165, 000 years, evidence is lacking that the Earth suffered cataclysmic upheavals during any of those intervals.

CHAPTER **38**

The Case for Ghosts

THOUGH GHOSTS SEEMED TO HAVE been here since our beginning, proving their existence, is difficult, like substantiating so much in this book. Shakespeare probably believed in ghosts, which doesn't necessarily validate them, although we tend to respect great minds. In his play, *Hamlet*, he depicts King Hamlet as a ghost before his son, Hamlet, and is careful to limit the King to a few words, which is consistent with centuries of eye-witnesses who supposedly encountered ghosts.

Rejecting that they exist because we've never seen one is like disbelieving a historical event because we weren't there when it occurred (or accepting only events that please us). Such rejection is like certain leaders of nations rejecting that the holocaust occurred, despite proof from pictures, documentation, and many eye-witness reports from survivors, including German officers and guards.

Because ghosts are often recognizable people, they usually appear where they suffered a traumatic experience, such as in a house, battlefield, or on a warship, et cetera. Since we cannot remain here in physical form after death because our body rots, I theorize that ghosts represent the spirits or souls of those that refused to accept death for many possible reasons and are struggling to prevail as humans.

They might have considered themselves too young to die, feared the consequences of hell as punishment for past sins, or refused to leave a loved one, and so on.

The souls of murdered victims, for example, could be struggling to remain here in order to seek justice or revenge. Still others might have lived such happy unstressed lives, that they refused to depart.

According to eyewitness reports, including photographs of ghosts, they usually resemble recognizable people, despite when they passed on, which supports the possibility that we probably retain our physical appearance in the next dimension. Surely countless near/death witnesses claiming to have recognized their relatives there, couldn't all be hallucinating, and/or lying.

Lacking enough energy (or whatever is necessary to sustain themselves), some ghosts might only be able to whisper, rather than speak, or can only materialize as vague apparitions. Whatever the case, trapped here, they could remain forever, unless or until they understand that they died, which often enables them to pass on.

Ghosts supposedly capable of causing major physical damage, as frequently portrayed in books or the movies, is doubtful. Most can't even close a door. Were they able to do much more, they could disrupt our laws and cause havoc, which doesn't occur.

Though I've never seen a ghost, I accept their existence because of such reports which include those from parapsychologists and reliable others, who couldn't all be hallucinating or lying either. Besides, the concept fits perfectly into my theory that they are souls of the departed that didn't reach the next world for reasons just cited.

CHAPTER 39

Analyzing Reincarnation

YEARS AGO, I ACCEPTED THE validity of reincarnation, a Hindu concept, much like I did the evolutionary theory, mostly because it became the trend and fashionable to do so. But even then, I recall doubting that we reincarnated through the insect and animal chain until our souls advanced enough to enter a human body, which seemed complicated and much like punishment. Besides, from God's standpoint, since most of us would lose whatever we learned in the past, why would God reincarnate the same soul repeatedly? That we are multiplying as humans that need souls, suggests that God is constantly creating them.

If reincarnating into low life forms were true, which would a soul enter first and why? Would it be an ameba or an ant? Considering that our soul is complicated, how could it enter such a microscopic organisms unless the Creator wiped out all that the soul knew, which would also be stupid?

If a soul entered an animal, when would it be ready to leave, choose another host, and, if so, which one? A turtle? Who decides, the soul? If God decided, that would be interference. In all the accounts that I have researched, those who supposedly remember bits of their former lives, never recall having been an animal or a microscopic organism.

Some contend that somehow our souls come from the mother and enter the baby's body shortly before or after its birth, which would imply that souls reside somewhere inside females. Another theory maintains that souls hover above a woman. But this would suggest that it resides outside of her, somewhere in the physical world, which would be also absurd, since it would be measurable, possibly even discernible.

I theorize that God creates souls in the spiritual world and they enter various bodies during specific moments in a woman's body.

Some believers claim that they are old souls who reincarnated many times, which is hard to believe, if they still possess serious faults. Ironically, I've noticed that such individuals seem quite wise and moral already. If so, why would they have reincarnated?

Were reincarnation true, all of us, not just a few, would remember some aspect of our former lives, including where certain incidents occurred and so on. But this would cause major problems. If those who hurt us, helped us, or were our lovers before, were still alive when we reincarnated and grew up, we would be tempted to seek revenge or try to resume our relationship with them, which would surely cause unnecessary problems.

Considering all those who supposedly remember bits of their former lives, I never met or read about anyone who admitted returning here in order to learn something new or reject a bad quality. Nor did anyone claim to have been a thief, rapist, or murderer, and so on, that is, those who would be most likely to reincarnate from their standpoint. Neither did anyone claim to reincarnate in order to help us invent something new for our benefit.

On the contrary, those who believe they reincarnated claim to have belonged to the aristocracy, nobility, or they were former movie stars, kings, queens, presidents, and even Jesus, which seems absurd, since, what would be the purpose of reincarnating, except to improve oneself, overcome past evils, and so on?

Curiously, considering all those who insist that they were scientists, great musicians, or artists, and so on during former lives, none seem to follow the same occupation after supposedly returning here.

Some reincarnation believers argue that we are not all permitted to reincarnate which would suggest favoritism and injustice again. In other words, in order to be fair and just, God would have to reincarnate everyone, including criminals and dictators like Hitler, Stalin, and Hussein, which would be stupid.

Some individuals, especially in India, have been able to describe accurately, who they were before, their former homes, and precise information about their supposed past lives, but they could simply be clairvoyant, or they could have somehow locked into someone else's former life which is possible under certain unusual circumstances.

Others claim that they were able to do so under hypnosis or while taking certain drugs. But if true, all of us should have that ability, which isn't happening.

I don't recollect having lived before and consider myself a new soul. In fact, very early in life I recall having trouble accepting that my awareness, my soul, was confined to a physical body. I also considered the insect world, animals, and plant life unusual, which provoked my almost insatiable curiosity. In other words, had I lived before, I should have recalled such life and not considered this world so strange.

CHAPTER **40**

The Soul Mate

BASICALLY, SOUL MATES ARE THOSE with whom we are most compatible, which could even include relatives, friends and those of similar sex. But like theories of evolution and reincarnation that catch our attention, this concept has snowballed.

Opposite sexes that resemble each other physically and spiritually sometimes believe that they're soul mates. Other supposed soul mates claim that they first met in the spiritual world and were like identical twins. A Hollywood version of soul mates depicts two lovers meeting again after passing on, reincarnating, and "living happily thereafter."

Despite how sincerely devoted we are to God and/or how often we pray for a soul mate, those who are serious about finding a soul mate or compatible partner need to do so on their own.

Those who believe that God answers such prayers need to consider the broader picture. How could a moral, loving, non-interfering Creator justify doing so, instead of helping millions who suffered and died during famines, natural disasters, wars, genocide, and so on since our beginning?

Finding a soul mate requires searching deeply within oneself through meditation (like praying, as I have maintained), in order to determine what qualities and attributes to prefer rather than others. Such reflection automatically prepares one to consider those who possess such qualities, rather than those who don't.

Meditating (praying) for a highly moral, loving soul mate, for example, would *probably* steer us away from liars, cheaters, and so on. I say *probably* because many other factors are involved, such as that opposites often attract. For example, sometimes we fall in love with the right person for wrong reasons or vice versa. We also could have met in order to help the other person or to exchange what the other has to offer us. The variations are endless. Because people change, finding a supposed soul mate isn't foolproof, much less that soul mates will remain together or compatible forever.

Since males and females might pray for the most beautiful or handsome, loving, moral partner respectively, which is only natural, finding that person is slim. Such souls might only exist in our fantasies, dreams or in the movies. Also, that soul could be involved with someone else or not part of one's destiny, and so on.

Staying at home (and waiting for that soul to knock on one's door) is too much like Hollywood and will reduce the chance of finding that special someone. Waiting for the Creator to make an exception in one's life, is wishful thinking. The point is, the more we include realistic qualities in the kind of soul mate that we long to find, the better is the chance of success.

CHAPTER **41**

God Answering me from the *Bible?*

I TOOK CAREFUL NOTES ABOUT the following unusual incident, including even the dialogue, which is as accurate as possible. Though I uphold many of the *Bible's* truths, it will contradict my criticisms of it. Excluding the incident, would have strengthened my criticisms about the *Bible*, but sharing my conception of truth with the reader is more important than where it leads me, and it stands for itself.

I don't rule out the possibility that the Creator could have influenced the prophets and other authors to include certain stories in the *Bible* while rejecting others. If this is true, they would have included their own personalities, that is, their fears, superstitions, and fantasies, which makes the *Bible* fascinating but controversial.

Billions of folks have read the *Bible* over the centuries. Many of us believe it's truly God's word. It has comforted, delighted, inspired, and frightened people. Many of us pray to God while holding it. Hotel and motel drawers often contain *Bibles*. We keep

Bibles in our houses thinking they will protect us from intruders and demons. We place a hand on *Bibles* in court and swear to tell the truth, which probably has frightened many of us into doing just that, and so on.

Despite the Bible's contradictions and half-truths, whatever the version, no other object or thing has received more handling or more spiritual energy from us over the centuries except perhaps, for the cross, which I theorize, has caused the object itself and/or the idea that it is God's word, to take on its own energy, whether spiritual, mystical, or both.

Whatever the case, before leaving to solo aboard the Royal Caribbean Cruise ship, *Mariner*, in May '07, I needed to buy a mixer for my synthesizer. I introduced myself to a bearded, young man who waited on me at a nearby music store, handed him my card advertising myself as a pianist, and we began talking. He had been studying theology all his life, particularly the *Torah* and *Old Testament* and planned to become a rabbi, he revealed, and I told him I was writing a book about metaphysics.

Still studying my card, he looked up. "I'm Adam."

Where's Eve? flashed a thought. "Now there's a name."

"I know."

"I just happened to be writing a chapter on the *Bible* right now."

He smiled curiously. "I'm not surprised."

What's that supposed to mean? crossed my mind.

"You have an Italian name. Were you born in Italy?"

"No. My parents were."

"You look like a Jew."

"I know. People often think I'm Jewish."

"It's no coincidence that we met."

My turn to smile curiously. Yeah, okay, I accept that possibility, I thought. So?

"You were probably a Jew in your former life."

Oh, here we go, I mused. "Really? How so?"

"During the Exodus, many Jews fled to Italy. I run into people like you, all the time. You've been guided to me like the others. You're searching for your identity, how you fit into the Jewish picture, why you're writing this book."

Now there's a wild theory if I ever heard one. Is he serious? I suppressed, eventually questioned him about the validity of the *Bible* which seemed to be a collection of fairy tales, and unloaded my major criticisms, that if it was truly God's word, how come such a supposedly loving and awesome intelligence that created the physical world and heaven, is often depicted as ruthless, unloving, demanding and even violent? "Surely, God doesn't need our rote praying, bowing, weeping, breast thumping and whatnot," I threw in, plus my criticism of the *Commandments.* I also complained about what I considered were important omissions, and began uncorking my list of recommendations, until he interrupted me.

"There's more to the *Bible* than you can imagine."

"So, if God influenced the prophets to write it, why did God make the *book* so hard for average folks to decipher?" I inquired and he mentioned the code.

"Even your name appears somewhere in the *Bible.*"

"You've got a great knack of avoiding my questions. No way. Impossible," I countered. "I'd have to see how you pull *that* off."

"I'll show you sometime," he tantalized. "But this isn't the time or place."

Eyeing several incoming customers, I realized the absurdity of such a philosophical discussion in a music store, sniffed out a laugh, and agreed.

"I'm quitting for good, tomorrow. You caught me just in time."

I smiled briefly, then frowned. Is he opening a door to different information for me? I reflected.

We agreed to trade email addresses before I left. I eventually bought a mixer, and he typed out my bill on his computer and printed it.

"You pay for this up front," he explained while examining it carefully and looked up. "It's got today's date, even the time, 3:14. Let's check that out."

What's he talking about? I wondered.

Turning back to the computer, he brought up the *Old Testament*, pulled up Exodus 3:14, and read me the passage. "Exactly what we were talking about."

Reading it, I frowned in surprise. "Coincidence," stumbled from my own lips, surprising me.

"Not really. Notice that 3:12 and 3:15 don't apply to our discussion at all."

Checking, I squinted in disbelief. He's right, I announced internally. "But what if that's not the correct time," squirted out carelessly from me. "I mean, what if the store's clock is off."

"Immaterial, man. Three fourteen came up. You rang and the Creator answered. Case closed. I told you there's more going on than you can imagine," he deposited upon my astonished face, left to get the mixer, and returned with it.

We exchanged more words, shook hands, and I left. Becoming my own devil's advocate, I found myself accepting the remote possibility that the *Bible* might somehow have been deliberately filled with contradictions and half-truths in order to attract continual attention to it, as it does for believers, non-believers, and even me that day.

CHAPTER 42

Nightmares and Demons

OUR CREATOR DIDN'T CREATE WHAT I will call *demons* for lack of a better word, nor does God sustain them which would be stupid and immoral. *We have,* in books and in the movies, often the most hideous the better. This includes creatures like the devil or Satan, various monsters, and so on, which we shouldn't ingest into the subconscious, why responsible parents often forbid their children to watch or read anything involving them.

I'm not implying that I haven't watched such movies, but I try to avoid them as much as possible, which isn't easy today, because we can't always predict what will unfold in a movie. Most amazing to me is how badly, that is, unrealistically (or stupidly), writers portray humans behaving even in family-orientated films. Aside from the usual violence, drugs, and sex, rather than dealing with meaningful issues involving average folks during physical life, most of today's films are trivial and superficial. They lack believable, realistic, opening conflicts, and usually concern the rich or the young who become rich and live in a mansion or they live in a beautiful home overlooking the ocean, drive a Mercedes or convertible, and have a boat on the side. Worse, they always have enough money to go anywhere, buy anything, and so on, which is too unreal, has no relevancy according to what is *really* going on in America and *is therefore boring.*

The point is, such beasts exist spiritually in our minds, which we carry into the next world after death. To repeat, ironically, if we somehow didn't create the devil and the flames of hell, et cetera here, such areas wouldn't exist there.

Superstitious and highly impressionable during elementary school, I associated demons with the devil, was unaware what they were, and worried that thinking about them was sinful. I also feared them, an attitude I continued to maintain even after I broke from the church.

During college, I remember concluding that believers in demons were ignorant and superstitious, but my attitude was destined to change, after I started teaching.

Desperately needing to stretch what little money I had just to buy food, during those difficult years, I had been resorting to petty thievery. Shopping at the local food store in our small town of under a thousand inhabitants, I remember never correcting any of the teenage cashiers for mistakenly undercharging me for groceries.

Since survey cameras were years away from being invented, when unobserved and before checking out, I would pocket a pen, hide similar small items in my cart, or stash cans of tuna inside a fifty pound bag of potatoes whenever I could afford to buy the large economy size.

I'm stealing so we can have enough food to feed my family and myself, I recall announcing inwardly, as if I were trying to justify myself or apologize to God. The store can afford to help me out anyway, I rationalized. Though I avoided getting caught, I admire stronger souls who never succumb to such temptations despite how poor or destitute they are. Nor did

I realize ironically, how little such petty thievery was *really* helping us financially.

One day, weeks into my first year teaching at the high school, I finally asked myself how I could justify stealing as a teacher, especially if I wanted to become a strong moral soul, as I had secretly hoped all my life. Often picturing how Christ refused the devil's temptation in the desert, as portrayed in the *Bible* (and elsewhere), I finally stopped stealing from then on. I also struggled to avoid lying (one of the most difficult so-called sins to overcome completely because human relations are involved, which are often complicated, although mostly because lying is often necessary in order to save money, true in my case.)

Still following Christianity and Christ's teaching, I continued treating others lovingly, including the unruly, which came natural to me. In fact, I sensed that I was a better Christian than most Christians who attended church and confession regularly.

As corny as this sounds, I even sneered at the devil. No one, not even he, one of the worst souls of all, could tempt me into reverting back to cheating, stealing, or lying, I proudly announced inwardly.

Although I had been experiencing nightmares throughout my life, I knew that everyone did occasionally, and I hardly dwelled on the matter. But when they continued throughout my teaching career, even during the long, restful Christmas breaks and after I began teaching better students, I was puzzled.

What am I doing wrong? I had begun to ask myself because I was generally positive, despite my economic woes. Rarely did I remain depressed long and although I was constantly practicing the piano and/or writing, I deeply appreciated that I had been blessed with talent (along with tremendous energy and fortitude), which had enabled me to improve both.

When the nightmares ensued even after I retired from teaching in 1985, I decided to change my lifestyle in hopes of ending them. I had long since stopped watching violent or horror movies on television. Though I had always been active indoors and out, I bought a set of used weights and began exercising religiously. I avoided eating meat and junk food and retiring with a full stomach, but without success. I tried hot tea and even milk, which I still disliked. Sometimes I even downed shots of liquor beforehand, but nothing worked, not even melatonin, aspirins, or special vitamins.

Though the nightmares were now unnerving me, I managed to shrug them off (because I had no other choice). In fact, waking in the morning, I always remained positive throughout the day. Nor did I ever imagine that they were related to my obsession to remain as morally impeccable as possible. In fact, I recall feeling so proud about being spiritual and moral, that one day I announced inwardly about striving to become as morally perfect as Jesus, and that did it. I started experiencing the worst nightmares ever, sometimes two per night, which stunned me, not because I thought Jesus was responsible, which I knew was impossible, since he was a great, loving, moral soul, but, rather, because I thought he would have somehow protected me.

Nor were these minor nightmares incidental, like those depicting me almost driving off a cliff or struggling to play on defective or weird pianos that lacked keys. Instead, they pertained to defecation, including relieving myself before strangers.

What's stimulating such revulsion? I demanded with frustration. Surely I wasn't responsible, I knew, since I wasn't masochistic, superficial, or negative. Nor did I blame God who I knew didn't interfere in our lives, much less was the Creator punishing me for stealing years ago. I have to tolerate such horror forever? I remember grumbling inwardly, mostly because I rarely experienced a pleasant dream.

They still plagued me when I started writing this book before I began soloing aboard the *Mariner* which left Cape Canaveral and returned to port there for two days after visiting the Caribbean Islands' east and west sides once a week.

Lounging on deck and viewing the fleeting ocean during the first two trips, I had appreciated relaxing and writing when I wasn't soloing, attending meetings, or participating in lifeboat drills. I had also enjoyed taking short breaks to visit the beautiful islands during the day. In fact, I had been so relaxed as the weeks passed, that days before my four month contract ended, I was thankful that the nightmares had stopped, *but only while we were at sea*, I suddenly realized. They always returned in full blast whenever we ported for two days in Canaveral, and *didn't write*, which puzzled me.

Being at sea away from land makes a difference? I asked myself after debarking and driving back home. But I was also so pleased about having written approximately fifty pages of this book during the cruise, that I dropped the matter again, although briefly. Absorbing another revolting nightmare while sleeping overnight at a motel in Virginia, I was jolted. What's going on? I protested inwardly again. I'm playing games with myself? Demons are responsible? I challenged inwardly for the first time, as I drove home. When another nightmare terrorized me that night after I unpacked and *didn't* write, I was dumbfounded. They also persisted during succeeding nights when I didn't write while attending to household matters and my large outside garden, just like whenever we ported for two days at Canaveral.

Demons are like the gremlins that supposedly plagued allied pilots during World War II? I considered, until I finally caught on to the pattern. They're haunting me when I *don't write*, I announced. But why? What's the connection? I demanded inwardly. Still unsure if that were *really* true, I decided to avoid writing the next day, angrily told them to get lost in so many words while I meditated, but to no avail. A terrible nightmare descended upon me that night.

If demons are responsible, why would they bother me when *I didn't write*? I queried again. How would I be able to write without ever taking a break in order to stop them? And why weren't good souls in the spiritual world suppressing them? I wondered.

Before I could unravel this dilemma, a familiar thought intervened. This is another *Catch-22*? We need evil souls in order to understand and learn the meaning and importance of loving one another because of the consequences that will follow if we don't? That's why the good souls have refused to intercede? I also considered. Then it hit me.

Demons or some negative energy appeared to be punishing me with nightmares because of who I have become and because I have been attacking such unknown negative entities throughout this book, much like how criminals or the mafia would respond against their enemies and the law.

But why would they when I *wasn't* writing this book? I struggled to understand, and, although hard to accept, harder to prove, and difficult to describe, I theorize the following, as fantastic and outrageous as this seems:

Connecting or communicating with good souls on the other side, or receiving their energy whenever I was writing this book, somehow blocked or prevented the demons from penetrating into my subconscious and giving me nightmares. Apparently, not writing this book broke my connection with the good souls, which enabled the demons to unload on me.

Did that mean that writing this book enabled me to defeat them or whatever had been responsible? I couldn't help thinking, as simple and once again as trite as this sounds, especially since, accept it or not, we're *really* involved in a battle between good and evil, whether here or in the spiritual world.

Apparently *they* did lose this battle because the book is alive. It exists in my computer, memory sticks and a cd, which I intend to send to my children. Even if I passed on before a publishing company accepted it, whatever had stimulated the nightmares wouldn't be able to destroy what I had saved.

Considering this a step further, as fantastic and superstitious as this sounds, demons or whatever might try to influence an agent or publisher to reject this book, which good souls would probably try to block, since it would be in their best interest to do so.

One way to prevent this and avoid months and even years of more rejection, was to try and pay to publish it, which would avoid having to deal with cocky, conceited agents, most of whom consider themselves superior to writers because of their connections with publishers, when, in fact, were it not for writers, they would have to work for a living. Nor would I waste more time catering to their nauseating insistence about how to write proposals, submit sample chapters, and so on, which they invariably reject anyway. (Thirty of them had already rejected the proposal for this book because, generally speaking, both lack imagination, and publishers would rather publish trash than take a chance printing a good book. In other words, money and/or what sells, rules what they publish. Nor was anyone interested that I had completed five other books, and my list of rejections is endless.) My only problem was how to raise the money without borrowing from anyone, which obviously happened.

Considering the energy or whatever negative unknowns penetrated my subconscious to cause my nightmares, they only lost this one battle. Surely nothing I have tried to convey through this book could annihilate them completely.

More incredible is that after close to five painstaking years devoted to writing and re-editing this book, I started having pleasant dreams, which I attribute to help from loving souls and praying to Jesus and the Father.

How readers will evaluate all this, might depend on the following incident which is proof enough for me. A month after finishing this book, I began re-editing "The Ouija Board Affair," a true but negative story involving the devil and/or possibly demons that I experienced with two other teens when we tried to summon some sign of the devil. Shortly after I finished re-editing this story,

I absorbed another typically outrageous, disgusting nightmare, which staggered me again.

At the risk of sounding gross, it involved defecation again. Naked in the nightmare (consistent with my open-mindedness and willingness to expose my most inner thoughts in writing in order to help others), I entered a men's room, noted two unidentified men (souls), and an odd, wooden stall that was painted red and had panel doors which I closed but couldn't lock. No sooner had I sat on the toilet in order to relieve myself, when one of the men opened the door in order to watch me. Something tried to bite me from underneath, and I woke up in the middle of the night. In other words, since I lost my connection with the good souls, demons were able to penetrate because, re-editing this particular story had given them access.

Today, I'm convinced that all this involved the spiritual aspect of us here and there, which is further proof for me that souls, their energy, or both, exist beyond physical life.

CHAPTER 43

Afterthought

DESPITE SO MUCH REJECTION AND suffering I endured throughout my life, all these experiences led to writing this book, which was my destiny, which I speculate was why I was born into the physical world. In fact, such thinking constantly crossed my mind during my life, which helped me to prevail, despite the odds. In fact, I accept that I was blessed with the talent and particularly the energy to do so, plus the talent to play the piano, which I theorize the good souls threw in as a gift. Nor can I rule out that they didn't inspire me to write this book.

Window required not just decades of reflection and writing millions of words, yes millions beforehand, especially because I do my own editing, but I had to master prose and poetry before I could do so. Nor should this book be confused with *Window of Eternity*, which cost me a fortune to have published (and edited) in 1984. Ironically, that book took less than a month to write in longhand, and I was amazed how little trouble I had organizing my thoughts and ideas, which is often a writer's nemesis. Evaluating that today,

I speculate that demons were controlling and maneuvering me to write what I speculate was mostly *their* ideas, not mine, which is called "automatic writing." Nor have I ever reread a single page of that book since then.

The moment I finished this book's first draft, I experienced the largest blue light ever in my left eye, why I chose the closest replica of it to appear on the front cover.

The bibliography that follows is important. Most of these books cite eyewitness who experienced the separation, the light, spiritual guides, and so on. In other words, although I listened to similar accounts from many others, I'm indebted to these authors for doing my fieldwork without realizing it.

Bibliography

Bernstein, Morey. *The Search for Birdie Murphy*. Garden City, New York: Doubleday and Co., 1956.

Bloomfield, Harold, M. D. *Transcendental Meditation*. New York: Dell Publication Co., 1975.

Castaneda, Carlos. *Journey to Ixlan*. New York: Simon and Schuster. 1973

Castaneda, Carlos. *The Teachings of Don Juan*. New York: Ballentine Books, 1969.

Evans-Wentz, W. Y., ed. *The Tibetan Book of the Dead*. New York: Oxford University Press, 1957.

Fuller, John. *The Ghost of Flight 401*. New York: Berkely Publishing Corp., 1978.

Hanford, James H., ed. *The Poems of John Milton*. New York: The Ronald Press Company, 1953.

Head, L. and Cranston, S. L. *Reincarnation: The Phoenix Fire Mystery*. New York: Julian Press/Crown Publishers, Inc., 1977.

Herrigel, Eugene. *The Method of Zen.* New York: Vintage Books, 1974.

Herrigel, Eugene. *Zen in the Art of Archery.* New York: Random House, 1971.

Jacobson, Nils O., M. D. *Life Without Death.* New York: Dell Publishing Co., 1973.

Klein, Aaron E. and Cynthia. *Mind Trips.* New York: Doubleday, 1979.

Kubler-Ross, Elisabeth. *On Death and Dying.* New York: Macmillan, 1969.

Monroe, James. *Journeys Out of the Body.* New York: Anchor Press, 1977.

Montgomery, Ruth. *A World Beyond.* New York: Coward, Mc Cann, and Geoghegan, 1971.

Moody, Raymond A., M. D. *Life After Death.* New York: Bantam Books, Inc., 1976.

Moody, Raymond A., M. D. *Reflections on Life After Death* New York: Bantam Books, Inc., 1978

Pearce, Joseph C. *The Crack in the Cosmic Egg.* New York: Pocket Books, 1973.

Rawlings, Maurice, M. D. *Beyond Death's Door.* Nashville: Thomas Nelson Inc., Publishers, 1978.

Ritchie, George. *Return from Tomorrow.* Lincoln, Virginia: Chosen Books, 1977.

Roberts, Jane. *How to Develop ESP Power.* New York: Frederick Fell, 1966.

Roberts, Jane. *The Seth Material.* Englewood Cliffs, New Jersey: Prentice-Hall, Inc., 1970.

Roberts, Jane. *Seth Speak.* Englewood Cliffs, New Jersey: Prentice-Hall, Inc., 1972.

Sagan, Carl. *The Cosmos.* New York: Random House, 1980.

Smith, T. V. *Philosophers Speak for Themselves.* Chicago, Illinois: The University of Chicago Press, 1952.

Steiner, Rudolf. *Knowledge of the Higher Worlds.* London: Rudolf Steiner Press, 1969.

Wambach, Helen. *Life Before Life.* New York: Bantam Books, Inc., 1979.

Way, The (The Living Bible). Wheaton, Illinois: Tyndale House Publishers, 1972.

Weiss, Jess E. *The Vestibule.* Port Washington, New York: Ashley Books, 1972.

Welch, Thomas. *Oregon's Amazing Miracle.* Dallas: Christ for the Nations, Inc., 1976.

World Book Encyclopedia, The 22 vols. Chicago: Field Enterprise Corp., 1974.